CUT

THE

EYEBALL

THE ULTIMATE SHORT BOOK ON WRITING SHORT SCREENPLAYS

By
Norith Soth

SHORT SCRIPT
GODS

www.shortscriptgods.com

Table of Contents

85 – AFTERWORD
Two Producer/CEOS who offer short film grants get the last word, because money talks and BS walks.

89 – FORMATICUS

I'M REALLY NOT TRYING TO GET THE LAST WORD. THIS HERE EPILOGUE IS FOR FORMAT, WHICH YOU DON'T REALLY NEED, RIGHT?.

Acknowledgements

I could not have written this book alone. It really began as an idea by my partner, Michelle Medvedoff. She pushed and encouraged me to write it. She fooled me into thinking I had a great to deal to offer on the topic and I believed her. "Well, there it is," the Emperor in "Amadeus"said. We have a book. I have to profoundly thank Mikhail Zislis for reading the book repeatedly and offering invaluable suggestions that amplified what you are about to read. I also want to thank Khayyam Kain, David Pendze, Matthew Helderman, Jonathan Marlow and Mark Lawyer for reading early drafts and confirming that I had something very exciting in my hands. It's very rare when everyone agrees you have something really good. "Cut The Eyeball" was one of those rare instances. Finally, I want to thank Diogo and the folks at "Red Raven" in Portugal who designed the awesome cover.

Introduction

In 1998, I was on a panel of five filmmakers who had made $10,000 films. At this time, making a film for 10k was considered next to impossible. And worse, it made no business sense; only Robert Rodriguez had achieved the impossible, getting studio distribution and launching a career with his 7k action film, "El Mariachi". Otherwise this was a doomed notion.

This was before HD, before it was respectable to shoot on digital, before iPhone cameras (hell, before cell phones became a normal part of existence). I was one of the naïve directors who, against all logic, borrowed and begged money to buy and develop 16mm film to, over the course of years, complete his or her first film.

Our debuts were pretty similar, most in black and white with bad sound, experimental storytelling, and years of labor; what we had in common was the desire to do it.

Of the filmmakers on the panel, I can only name one film you may or may not recognize (that filmmaker was timid and didn't speak much). When the panel descended to the last question, via a woman who paid to attend it, it was something along the lines of, "what do you think making this film will do for you?"

Strangely, none us could answer. There was a fog of silence in the room, like we had all been caught doing something wrong. We knew it was a positive experience, but we were tongue tied. Had we had all been too obsessed to consider this end game? That it could all amount to nothing? What *did* we expect from our films?

One of the filmmakers may have replied that he didn't know, but he was glad he did it. The panel ended very negatively, dissolving into a cautionary tale rather than the inspiring exhibition of filmmakers IFP West had promised.

Like Jason Alexander in "Seinfeld", only an hour went by before I had an entire soliloquy in my head about how making my film was the greatest experience, blah, blah, blah, and only good things had come out of doing it. I have since fantasized of professing a Malcolm X-like inspirational speech about the creative empowerment of doing your own production. Everyone applauds in the end. They leave determined to make their own 10k movie. In reality, it was the worse ending to a filmmaking panel I had ever been a part of, either as audience or speaker.

My film did get distribution; two midnight screenings at Laemmle's Sunset 5, one screening at Panavision in Tarzana. Today, "Beyond The Screen Door," an adaption of Franz Kafka's "The Metamorphosis," is available on DVD through Pathfinder Pictures and on streaming via Fandor.

I never made my money back. "Beyond" did not launch my career, but it didn't end it. I continued making films either as a writer, producer or director and today, my job is mainly that of a professional screenwriter. I can say, without being full of crap, that I am paid to write scripts. Did making "Beyond" help me in anyway? Sure, every experience builds, especially the first. I can't honestly answer how, but it did.

However, that question, "what do you think making this film will do for you?" is today the seminal question you have to ask yourself before embarking on any filmmaking adventure. The proper translation being the ever-parental question, "how do you expect to make money from this endeavor?" This was the smoking gun. It was perfect. And the answer was actually right in front of the woman who asked it. The problem was, like many things in life, it would not be answered until a later time. Two years, to be exact.

Remember the timid filmmaker? The director of the film you may or may not recognize? Title of that guy's film was "Following" (made for 6k, filmed in black and white, fractured storytelling, and years of labor). Two years later, this guy made a movie called "Memento" and five years after that, "Batman

Begins." In the 17 years since that panel, Chris Nolan successfully launched his career as a result of making his cheap, 16mm movie, most recently with his $200 million opus, "Interstellar".

Nolan was one of the six filmmakers in the panel – and the straw that broke the camel's back. The perfect role model, answering loud and clear the question, "what do you think making this film will do for you?"

With "Memento", the Camelot of microbudget arrived into the new millennium. With the advent of HD, people now believed they could make a really cheap movie and succeed in Hollywood... and as it was said in the Old Testament, "this was good." Even established directors like Richard Linklater, Brian De Palma and especially Steven Soderbergh got into the mix. Why do I bring up this story about feature films in relation to the short screenplay book in your hands?

Because, in 1998, there was no model, and very little financial motivation, for making a $10,000 film in 16mm; that model eventually materialized. Much like short films today.

There isn't a clear path to making an income from shorts, there isn't the proper distribution and so on – but there will be. How do I know this? Supply and demand. Simple as that. We like our stories short. We watch films on tablets, just as our children watch cartoons on tablets. Hollywood films average two and half hours, not including commercials, and many of us don't have that kind of time or money to burn. The price of a movie ticket goes up every year, whereas the quality of story lessens every year. The "virtual campfire," the place where we find out stories, are mostly on the web.. YouTube, Vimeo, Netflix, Fandor, HULU, etc.

This is where the New Chris Nolan will emerge, a director of rich, engaging short films that enriches audiences worldwide. His films will be 45 minutes in length, properly financed, cast with major actors, written by major writers. His works will be anticipated. His stories will be talked about and emulated. The New Chris Nolan could be you. How do I know? Because he has not emerged yet, therefore he could be any of you.

The only thing in your way is not money or resources, but a story, a short screenplay. A blueprint that represents your vision, your point of view in sound and picture. You have often fantasized the events, the characters, what they say, what they wear, the music, the architecture. You just don't know how to harness it, control it, tame it on paper.

This is my trade. People hire me to write their shorts everyday. They either tell me, "I have the idea, I just don't know how to write it" or "I want to write a short, I just don't know."

This book was written to free you from the false notion that you "don't know" how to design your short screenplay. By the end of this book, you will be very aware that you are in control of your filmmaking destiny. The decision to make your short, to determine if you are the Next Chris Nolan, will come down to one single person – you!

THE CENTER OF GRAVITY

If you were fighting a war, you would figure out your enemy's greatest weakness – then, exploit that. In this little war, *you* are your enemy. Your doubts, fears and relentless analysis are the soldiers, barb wires and machine guns firing *at* you. During the course of this book, I will, piece by piece, detonate all the doubts, fears and pointless analysis. I will smart bomb the bunker where your enemy lives. When the smoke clears, I will introduce you to a person very capable of designing his/her first short film.

This is not a book about production. There are many books and blogs that will offer great advice about every facet of filmmaking. You can learn how to make a film just by listening to Robert Rodriguez's bravado "El Mariachi" DVD commentary. I'm not interested in writing a book that already exists. Tons of material exists about lighting, camera, editing, promoting, what I have not seen is an engaging book about the "center of gravity" – The short screenplay. The story. The most glaring absence in the "virtual campfire." Without it, you can't make your film.

"What about money?" you wonder.

I lived during an era where, without money, you could not make a film. At that time, you had to rent a camera, a Nagra recorder, boom mike, huge lights, electrical wires, you needed to develop your film and rent a flat bed for editing. Without a Santa Clause bag of cash, you could not do it.

Today, that is *no longer* the case. You can produce a film on your iPhone and get into Sundance. Because of how tiny and inconspicuous cameras are, its not difficult to steal a location. Your iPhone even records decent sound. It's simply not reality to believe money is the issue. You likely have most of the things you need right now. What you don't have is The. Short. Screenplay. A short story from within you, translated into sound and picture, ready to film. That is your center of gravity.

Now, the facet of the Chris Nolan story you want to observe is… he made a feature film. Not a short. Nolan needed to construct a full length screenplay, which is hell to write. A marathon of the mind. A Tour de France of the soul. Anguish, pain, a harmony of left and right brain. Torture, damnation, a place no man, woman or child should be. It could take years to write a good one. Good news! You're not writing a full length screenplay – you're writing a *short screenplay*!

Aaaah, the short screenplay, she breathes, she dances unhindered. I worship her. She is sexy, she is easy, she is short!

If writing a feature screenplay is making Thanksgiving Meal, writing a short screenplay is making lemonade.

THE UPLOADER VS. THE STORYTELLER

Since Luis Bunuel and Salvador Dali wrote "Un Chien Andalou" in 1926, cinema has never been the same. The shot of a woman's eyeball getting cut by a razor blade has never been forgotten. No short film since has topped it (Gaspar Noe's "Carne" comes close).

That doesn't mean *you* can't cut the eye ball – meaning, make a short film with such cathartic power, everyone is talking about it.

This is certainly a great time in history for the short film. The web is not only a sprawling spice market of short films, it is the greatest library of human expression ever. Whether that is a good or bad thing has yet to be determined. What we do know is, this is "virtual campfire" where people seek out their stories.

Everyone and their mother, literally, are YouTubing or Vimeoing a short narrative. *Everyone and their mother* has access to high quality HD. But *everyone and their mother* are not storytellers. They just shoot stuff. And upload it. They are *uploaders*. Perhaps this footage has meaning for some. Perhaps, this footage was not easy to acquire. I'm not here to devalue uploaders. I'm illustrating the difference between telling a story versus sharing raw, unedited footage.

This where *you* come in. You are a storyteller. You want to use the "virtual campfire" to express yourself. That's a huge difference.

As different as a Crip and a Blood.

As different as a Capulet and a Montague.

As different as "Survivor" and "True Detective." You fancy yourself *a filmmaker*. Paul Thomas Anderson, Martin Scorsese, Woody Allen, Katheryn Bigelow, that kind of filmmaker. Your goal is not to shoot footage of woman tripping over a barrel of wine. You have something *to say*. Something to release *from within*. The film medium is your kindred spirit and you're ready to demonstrate this to the world. Maybe you want to tell the story of the woman that fell, make a short film about the recurring nightmare she suffered, after being globally humiliated. You want the tragedy, the human essence, the story of triumph over Cabernet, not the sound byte.

The difference between you and the uploader is one thing – *a short screenplay.* When you complete this book, the locomotion of writing a short screenplay will be imprinted in your mind. I wrote this book for you.

You may also be an uploader who is a closet storyteller. Maybe the footage you capture, you want to concentrate into a shorter narrative, make it more compact and sophisticated – you want your audience to understand your unique point of view. In that case, I wrote this book for you too.

Look, I wrote this book for anyone who desires to use the film medium as a short narrative to tell a story. Film students, high school students, senior citizens, someone who's thought about doing this for years, or someone who just needs a hobby. If you're interested in reaching a high form of storytelling in the short form, I will lead you to the promise land – and perhaps, you too will cut the eyeball!

I'VE BEEN THERE

Remember the beginning of "Rosemary's Baby" when Roman Castavet said, "I've been everywhere. You name a place and I've been there. Go ahead, name a place." Someone says, "Fairbanks, Alaska!" Roman replies,"I've been there, all over Alaska. Fairbanks, Juneau, Anchorage, Nome, Sitka, Seward."

Well, that's pretty much me when it comes to screenwriting. I've *been there*. In my 20+ years in the film industry, I've written every script imaginable. Action, comedy, thriller, horror, romance, weird, dark comedy, family, artsy, cartoons, children's stories, corporate, mockumentary, commercials, infomercials, infographics, you name it, *I've been there*. I've sold scripts, had them optioned, and even was part of some productions. I've worked with people like Justin Lin (director of "Fast and Furious 3-6" and the upcoming "Star Trek Beyond"), Norman Reedus ("The Walking Dead"), Stephen Chin ("Gummo," "Play It to the Bone") and Brad Miska ("V/H/S"). I'm not Shane Black, but I make a living as a screenwriter. Most importantly, I've endured every screenwriting scenario you can think of and conquered it. Writer's block, procrastination, writing with a tight deadline, writing with no deadline, writing when I absolutely do not feel like it, writing something I hate, writing with structure, writing with no structure, writing more than one script simultaneously, name the situation and *I've been there*.

I also lend my screenwriting skills *outside* Hollywood. I've written scripts for film students, teachers, corporations, web filmmakers. I've written with every sex, race, age and creed all over the world. Muslims, Christians, Republicans, Liberals, Russians, Jews... I have seen every point of view out there. During the last few years, my workload for short films has increased insanely. Everyday, someone has an idea for a short film but has no clue how to begin writing it. There's a traffic jam of people with ideas who don't realize they can create the blue print to their short film as easily as making lemonade.

I'm tired of seeing people postpone making their shorts for months (or years!) because they don't believe they can write one. Like most fears, its exaggerated. Like most things you can't do for yourself, the problem is *yourself*. When you realize how easy it is to write a short script, you will amaze yourself and write it – and then you will film it. It doesn't matter if you're doing this for a career, for creative expression or to *find out* if you're the New Chris Nolan. It doesn't cost a boat load of money anymore.

I'm here to show how to write a short screenplay. It's not only *easy*... it's fun and liberating. While I love cats, I can't stand the idea of another cat video. What I'd like to see is cat movies! Cats in stories, not in Musicals or in a home video, but taking part in a story.

Okay, what's the first part of making lemonade? Getting the ingredients. You can't just say, I'm going to make lemonade and expect lemons, sugar, and water to appear magically. You have to go buy it at the store.

Let's go shopping...

PART I - THE WWW RECIPE

There are only two parts to this book. This is the first. This is the only part you will actually need (second half is the training wheels). We're gathering ingredients to make lemonade but there's one problem. We all have different tastes. Some like it sweet, others like it sour, while others enjoy it with extras like mint leaves.

Your short film idea, concept or the just basic desire to make a short will come to fruition with The WWW Recipe, a practical formula, consisting of three basic questions.

1. Who the hell are you?
2. Why the hell are you making it?
3. What the hell are you making?

WHO THE HELL ARE YOU?

Yes, who the hell are you to even think about making a short? Let's see, you're a member of the human race in the year 2015. Everyone on Earth has access to some kind of device that records events. Your species spend about 70% of their time reviewing recorded material on said devices. Lots of times, this material is atrocious or godawful (but people watch it anyway).

However, you see a higher meaning in this freedom of expression. You want to say something. You want to make something unique. You want to create something, dare I say, *transcendent*. It's *in* you and you must get it out. Because, you are one of these seven freaks of nature.

The Visionary

You have a vision. You see images in your head. This is so vivid, you are obsessed. A man falling out of a window. A shoe walking without a body. A dog smiling. An image blooms in your mind and you want to see how far and wide it mushrooms. You must bring this vision to life. Somehow.

If only it made sense. You could then write it.

MISCONCEPTION: Shorts films don't have to make sense! "Un Chien Andalou" makes zero sense. Luis Bunuel had a dream about a cloud slicing the moon in half "like a razor blade slicing through an eye." His buddy Salvador Dali countered with his own dream about "a hand crawling with ants." The two Spaniards wrote a short screenplay and proceeded to make the film in 1928. The film became what the late Roger Ebert called "the most famous short film ever made" and then added, "anyone who is halfway interested in cinema sees it sooner or later, usually several times... it is an ancestor of today's independent digital movies." Did I mention this review was written 72 years later?

Visionaries must free the river of images from their minds. And there's no better medium than the short film to do this with. Luis Bunuel's career never looked back after "Un Chien Andalou." Luis has 6 films in Sight and Sound's prestigious top 250 films of all time. His films somehow got better as he got older. He followed his vision. Always. Follow the bread crumb of your vision, the Bunuel Way.

Famous Visionaries: Michel Gondry ("Human Behaviour"), Benh Zeitlin ("Glory At Sea"), Tim Burton ("Frankenweenie").

The Pragmatic

You're dying to make a film, but you don't have anything. Except three room mates, a toaster, a microwave oven, and two suits. Oh wait, now that you think of it, your Uncle has a liquor store and the subway your ride to and from work has no security guard.

Speaking of work, you have the keys to the office where you work, and only the janitor shows up at night. His name is Clyde.

MISCONCEPTION: Wait a minute, you do have something! Many somethings! Roommates, toaster, suit, a subway, an office and Clyde. You can't wrap a movie around that? Ever heard of a guy by the name of George Lucas?

George had this crazy idea that you could make "a futuristic movie using existing stuff." His opportunity came when USC asked him to teach a film class to members of the US Navy (an icky obligation. Navy students were hotheats and misbehaved in class).

But young Lucas' eyes lit up when he learned the Navy paid for unlimited film and lab processing costs for their students! BINGO! Lucas green lit his own short and made his Naval students the cast and crew of his short "Electronic Labyrinth THX 1138 4EB."

Plus, the US Navy affiliation granted him access to locations at LAX, the Van Nuys Airport, the USC Computer Center and other very forbidden places that looked futuristic. Most of the shooting was done on nights and weekends. And indeed, the short film that catapulted George Lucas' career was made. We all pretty much know what happened next. All because Lucas was privy to what he could use from his environment. It's time to call up Clyde.

Famous Pragmatics: Robert Rodriguez ("Bedhead"), Jean-Luc Godard ("Operation Beton"), Francis Coppola ("The Two Christophers").

The Comic Genius

You're hilarious. Everything that comes out of your mouth is crazy and funny. People are all over the floor whenever you say anything. You can't so much as breathe without your friends pissing their pants laughing. What's not funny is, you're dying to make a movie but you're too busy telling jokes to write 5 pages of screenplay.

MISCONCEPTION: Comedy is one of the greatest weapons of cinema. Comedians have channeled this ability since movies were born. Charlie Chaplin, Jerry Lewis, and the ultimate critic's darling, Woody Allen, have taken complete advantage of their ability to make people laugh. Trey Parker's comic genius won him a Student Academy Award with the short, "American History," and he just made the movie for his class. Harness your mind-blowing sense of humor into a short screenplay, like Trey Parker and Matt Stone did with "Jesus vs. Santa," and you're as golden as a golden shower.

Famous Comic Geniuses: Mike Judge ("Milton"), Ben Stiller ("The Hustler of Money"), Mel Brooks ("The Brewmaster").

WARNING: It could save time to not falsely believe you're a "comic genius." I mean, it's your first short, you know best, but you may feel better about yourself if you know you're not particularly funny, but want to do something "comedic" anyway. This is actually an advantage, known as...

The Dry Comic Genius

You're not hilarious. People don't laugh with you, they laugh at you. Doesn't matter, you're a closet clown. That is, you have an eye for tragedy. Like the tragedy of living at home, even though you're 28. Or the tragedy of being late to the Apple Store when they're giving away the new iPhone. Or, the worst tragedy, desiring to make a short film with no experiences to draw from. You're not funny, but your older sister at Yale is a riot. Is there a short movie in this?

MISCONCEPTION: OMG, there's such a short movie in this. Sundance kills for this type of short film. Since Jim Jarmusch and

Whit Stillman became legends for trailblazing dry goods comedy, filmmakers have been falling all over themselves trying to harness melancholy in a bottle.

Wes Anderson and The Duplass Brothers have become self-made industries of sand paper humor, simply by squeezing out "that's funny" moments from any situation (you know, when you say "that's funny" but don't laugh?). Call it dramedy, mumblecore, Charlie Brown, it's all the same. They all began with the short film and now they own HBO.

Famous Dry Comic Geniuses: Jared Hess ("Peluca"), Wes Anderson ("Bottle Rocket"), Duplass Brothers ("This is John").

The Next Scorsese

You love the camera more than your own mother. You have been pre-visualizing a style in your head forever. When you walk on the streets, you see shots moving around pedestrians, cars, dogs, up and down buildings. You see cuts. Dissolves. You are the Next Scorsese, Brian DePalma or Rainer Werner Fassbinder. Like them, you see A Film By You or a You Picture in huge block letters and great reviews. You just don't see a screenplay.

MISCONCEPTION: Alfred Hitchcock drew his scripts, then hired a screenwriter to fill in the blanks. There's no hard rule, but get this, cinema is a visual medium. VISUAL. Gaspar Noe's "Carne" clearly has a "cinematic voice." Next Scorseses are visual novelists. Without the film medium, they would perish, then cease to exist. Their voice is purely cinematic and thus, the creation of a screenplay is the natural next step.

Famous Next Scorseses: Spike Lee ("Joe's Bed Stuy Barbershop: We Cut Heads"), Kathryn Bigelow ("The Set-Up"), Darren Aronofsky ("Supermarket Sweep").

The Dialogue Diva

You've probably written your short, but it's like 53 pages long. And all dialogue. Quentin Tarantino is one of the few geniuses working in cinema today, but the worse influence in cinema history. He does it so well, *Everyone and their mother* thinks they can write tons of dialogue. But you can't help it, you love writing dialogue (if you were in a mental hospital, you'd just write dialogue on walls with your own feces). You can't even see the 5 page script you intended to write, because it's buried in weeds of dialogue.

MISCONCEPTION: A person deeply in love with their own dialogue may not understand that dialogue divas like Tarantino or Judd Apatow are genre filmmakers. They pick their genre, then wrap miles of dialogue around it. In Tarantino and Apatow films, there is usually lots of tension as a result of genre commitment. Both of these guys employ "The Secret Mystery" or "The Forbidden Love" (a benefit of genre commitment). You will learn about these devices and thus your golden dialogue will have a wonderful sheen, like Martin McDonagh's Oscar winning short, "Six Shooter."

Famous Dialogue Divas: Paul Thomas Anderson ("Cigarettes & Coffee"), Eric Rhomer ("Journal d'un scélérat"), Sofia Coppola ("Lick The Star").

The Self-Muse

You look amazing. Every time you catch a reflection of yourself, you are intoxicated. You're not *just* super attractive. Your ability to telegraph human emotions is astonishing. The mere raising of the eyebrow says this or a slight smirk says that. The only muse you need is yourself. But no one seems to understand this. They think you're full of it. Weird. You're only trying to share what you see in the mirror with the world. How can that be selfish? You're the most generous person alive. If only someone would write you a script.

MISCONCEPTION: Many actors in history were masters at creating their own vehicles to "muse" off themselves. William Shakespeare was an actor who always wrote himself parts. Orson Welles is considered by many the best filmmaker in history; he "mused" himself without shame. Warren Beatty was once so enamored with himself, he would spend hours combing his eye lashes, and somehow still found time to scribble screenplays for great films like "Shampoo" and "Bulworth." Sylvester Stallone wrote "Rocky" and took a fraction of his screenwriting fee to star in it, because he couldn't live in a world where "Rocky" did not star Sylvester Stallone (and neither can you, admit it).

In the world of shorts, you only need to look at "Meshes In the Afternoon" by Maya Deren to understand the height of this skillset. Deren never took credit for starring in her films, but it's obvious she acted as her own muse. She used the ability to constantly fall in love with herself to a new level, pushing the boundaries of cinema to its greatest heights. A dancer, she pushed the camera on her body, her arms, her feet, her way of moving. Your fearless willingness to share your own reflection with the world can do the same.

Famous Self-Muses: Vin Diesel ("Multi-Facial"), Lena Dunham ("Creative Nonfiction"), Billy Bob Thornton ("Some Folks Call It a Sling Blade").

DUAL TYPES

It's possible that you could see yourself in two of these types. Like being Capricorn born in late December, or having a Jewish Mother and a Catholic Father.

For instance, Lena Dunham can be categorized as The Dry Comic Genius and a Self-Muse. David Lynch is a Visionary and Pragmatic. Maya Deren is not only a Self-Muse, but a Next Scorsese (even though Scorsese was in diapers when she was making films). You get it. Think of it as a having a major and minor.

Just remember, there's only *one major*. That's the one you want to focus on. For instance, if you're a Self-Muse, you want to create a script that takes advantage of your luscious features above all else. This takes us to the second W...

WHAT THE HELL ARE YOU MAKING?

Just as there were 7 types of filmmakers, there are only 6 types of short films you could be making. Whether you're establishing a career, desire to use the medium as a creative expression, or you just want to do it to see if you can do it, sharply focusing on one of these types will liberate you even further.

The Genre Short

Comedy, drama, thriller, horror, action-adventure. It doesn't get more specific than this. You've been exposed to them since birth. The genre movie gives you the freedom to explore your creativity in its concrete pillars. A comedy is funny (great for The Comic Genius or Dialogue Diva), a Drama is tragic (great for the Self-Muse or Dry Comic Genius), a thriller is exciting (great for The Next Scorsese), horror is scary (great for The Visionary), action-adventure is fun (great for The Pragmatic). You can also gauge how a genre may not fit your archetype.

For example, The Self-Muse may think twice before doing action. The Comic Genius may think twice before doing a Drama. The Dry Comic Genius may think several times before doing a thriller. You get it. Know thyself. If you're really delusional, ask your friends what your strengths are (just don't pose it like this: "I'm really funny, right?").

Genre is a safe way to go. Very difficult to mess up. The very first film every made was a Genre Movie, "The Great Train Robbery," an Action-Adventure made in 1903 by director, Edwin S.Potter. Today, this short film remains a 10-minute tour-de-force.

The Weird Short

Imagine if Hollywood promoted "weird movies." You go into a meeting and pitch "Sleepless in Seattle" meets "Die Hard." Studio head says,"you have a greenlight it if its *Sleepless* meets *Die Hard* meets *Child's Play.* "

Wait a minute, there's a long distance romance where the man fights terrorist in corporate building... led by possessed doll? That is weird. But you're visionary, you're straightening out your beret, thinking, *very interesting.*

Weird movies are extremely common in the short film universe (as common as the thriller or rom-com in Hollywood). We are talking about a medium that lends itself to logic forgiveness, because it's *short,* like poetry or music (poems and song lyrics are, more often than not, surreal and make zero sense). Bottom line, unlike feature films, weirdness has no shame in shorts – in fact, it's encouraged! Since forever, short films have become popular or even made careers, as we know with "Un Chien Andalou."

You can even go back to Georges Méliès' "A Trip to the Moon" and "The Impossible Voyage" to find how accepted these Weird Shorts were to a commercial audience in 1903 (as seen in Scorsese' film, "Hugo").

David Lynch began his career making Weird Shorts like "The Grandmother" and never stopped, practically inventing his own genre by staying weird. Animated films (cartoons, puppetry, stop motion such as the great shorts of Jan Svankmajer and The Quay Brothers) are often weird, as their narrative lends itself to stream-of-consciousness imagery.

You want to see weird? Check out the brilliant Russian short "The Cameraman's Revenge," a story of infidelity with dead bugs as actors. Don't you see, the very weirdness is the reason why you want to put this book down and see it.

In the Eighties, Weird Shorts spawned an entire culture. From Madonna's burning crosses in "Like a Prayer" to Peter Gabriel's stop motion "Sledgehammer" to Michael Jackson's "Thriller," the

Music Video ruled Television – for five minutes, a hit song would accompany a sequence of images that rarely made sense.

Today, former music video directors David Fincher, Spike Jonze and Michel Gondry are three of the most sought after directors in Hollywood. Yes, it definitely pay$ to be weird.

The Spoof

The Spoof is one of the most common career propellers in movies. There is a simple reason for this. The Spoof uses the popularity of a pre-existing film and makes fun of it. In the 80's, Ben Stiller made a 10-minute short, spoofing Scorsese's "The Color of Money." Stiller played a bowling shark (instead of a pool shark) in "The Hustler of Money." The Oscar winning short "West Bank Story" (Produced by my friend Pascal Vaguelsy) cleverly spoofed "West Side Story" but substituted the East-West neighborhoods of New York for the "West Bank" in Israel.

Matt Stone and Trey Parker have employed "The Spoof" relentlessly and shamelessly (till this day, "South Park" episodes spoof pre-existing media and that's why we love them). It's a genre that "The Comedic Genius" is very attracted to, for obvious reasons. A true comedian is a critic of society. He or she holds up a mirror to the absurdity they see and you go, "ha, ha, ha!"

While "The Spoof" lends itself to comedy, Visionaries like Tim Burton have also employed it successfully. After making his Frankenstein spoof (with a dog instead of a man), Burton was sought after by all the studios ("Frankenweenie" has since been remade into a feature).

The Autobio

It's not necessary to spill your guts about your sex life (though, for a Self-Muse, that's not a bad idea) or to give up the story of your horrible childhood in 5 minutes (though, for a Next Scorsese, that's not a bad idea.) You just need *something* that has happened to you - an event, a horrible moment, a destroyed romance, a stressful job, and make a short film about it. We're talking, one moment, maybe two.

The genuine article is unmistakable. Audiences can sense when something is real. This is why Robert DeNiro gained 38 lbs for "Raging Bull" or Nicolas Cage ate a cockroach in "Vampire's Kiss." When an audience is told a story, they desperately want to believe, "this is real." It's called "suspension of disbelief."

For you, the short film auteur, dramatizing a real life experience is a convenient way to achieve this "suspension of disblief." That's why, the Autobio can be gold.

Mark and Jay Duplass spent 65 grand to make a feature, which was so bad, it's still not seen today. Depressed and questioning why they were alive, the bros saw only one way out of this mess – make another movie. Immediately. Mark told Jay he was going to get their film equipment and to think of an idea by the time he got back.

Jay came up with a mini-nightmare he endured earlier that day, recording his voice in his answering machine over and over and over and over again until he wanted to tear the hair out of his head. The short, "This is John" got the bros into Sundance, SXSW and now they have their own show on HBO. The Autobio is an all you can eat buffet for The Dry Comic Genius and The Dialogue Diva.

The Twilight Zone Short

There is no greater example of gripping short narrative like Rod Serling's brilliant TV show, "The Twilight Zone." Although Seling's show was weird, it was more than that. Cautionary tales and social and political commentaries were frequently at the heart of the revolutionary program. "Twilight Zone" episodes were never weird for weird's sake (there's nothing wrong with that, of course, but that's a different category). This genre is ripe for Next Scorseses, as it frequently lends itself to unique cinematic style. Innovative techniques are frequently seen in "The Twilight Zone Short" to demonstrate a nightmare world where the protagonist is trapped, usually by society. Maya Deren's "Meshes In the Afternoon" is such film, but the most popular may be Chris Marker's "La Jetee," perhaps the most influential short in modern cinema.

Marker told the entire story, using still photographs and bravado sound design. 20 years later, it was made into "The Terminator" and 10 years after that into "12 Monkeys."

The Mock (or Mockumentary)

The Mock is a fake documentary. Made up reality, in the guise of news footage, found footage, or just a movie that has every facet of a documentary but isn't. Orson Welles became the father of this genre when he read "War of the Worlds" on the radio like it was a news program, freaking out Americans and changing the law forever. "Citizen Kane" may contain the first fake documentary, opening with a deceptively good news reel.

Thanks to Welles, the FCC insists you have to tell your audience a radio program is fake when it's fake – but in film, there is no such law.

This may be the reason why The Pragmatic is so attracted to the Mock. "Alive, in Joburg" may perhaps be the most popular of these shorts. Neil Blomkamp mixed lo-fi with visual effects to create the short mockumentary that got Peter Jackson's attention and famously became "District 9." All over the world, this *UFO in the sky* short materializes, usually followed by millions of YouTube hits. Visual effect skills are very accessible in our time. If George Lucas began his career today, he wouldn't need the US Navy to do it, he wouldn't have to leave his apartment.

Dry comic geniuses like Christopher Guest ("This Is Spinal Tap," "Best In Show") have not been shy about using The Mock. Woody Allen began his directing career with "Take The Money and Run" and subsequently made "Zelig" and "Husbands and Wives." All Mocks.

This is the method actor version of the short. The medium itself believes it's real. Fun to make and design. Limitless possibilities. We have not even scratched the surface with Mocks. "Found footage" films have gotten bad raps because of "The Blair Witch Project" (a great Mock that taught all the wrong lessons). But get this, The Mock is the only genre where you can do the craziest stuff under the guise that the footage is "found" or "pre-existing."

One of the best shorts I've ever seen is Mikal Britt's "The Last Happy Meal" about a teenage girl agreeing to do a snuff film.

Now that you know who the hell you are and what the hell you're making, let's tackle the last W...

WHY THEY HELL ARE YOU DOING THIS?

We are almost there. This final W will tighten the focus and free you to design your short film masterpiece. By now, you should have good portion of your lemonade ingredients. There's only one missing, but which?

Just as the first question had 7 answers, the second had 6, this one has 5, lending us the spirit of a countdown (7-6-5-4-3-2-1)... to you making your short film!

THE FILM STUDENT FILM

You've been going to school since you were five. Elementary, middle school, high school and now film school! You're either wealthy or up to your neck in debts (don't blame me, I only charged you three bucks). What you don't have is a short film because you don't have a short screenplay because you have not written one.

Bottom line: The lack of a short script in your life is a problem. There's a lot at stake. A degree. Impressing your parents who helped you pay for the tuition. Outdoing the turtlenecked jerk in your class who appears limitlessly talented (and connected).

You've tried writing your short. You keep putting it off. Your screenplay professor sounds like he's talking another language. A writing partner has been no help. Sceenwriting books talk about features, but you just need 5 or 10 pages. If only there was a book on just writing short scripts..

THE SUMMER MOVIE

Summer is a symbol of free time. The idea is, you'll have enough leisure to engage in a creative project – building a cabinet, writing a book, playing your guiatr or making a short film. Problem is, you're an adult now and you work year round. Fall, winter, spring and summer are all the same. The seasons are rotating viciously and if you don't make a move soon, you will be stuck doing whatever job you're doing until you're dead (or you'll get laid off and find another job you hate doing until you're dead). By *move*, I mean, *a movie*. A short movie that demonstrates the God-given talent you're dying to demonstrate to the World.

Whereas money is the enemy of "The Film Student Film," time is the enemy of "The Summer Movie." You've always been serious about a career in cinema, you just can't find the time to create the amazing blue print to your career defining short film. It's time to make your "Summer Movie" now, regardless of what time of the year it is or how old you are. If you're kid, make a short film while you still have summers. They don't last forever. Now, if only there was a book explaining how to write a short script?

THE DRUNK $5 MOVIE

So, you're getting together with some buddies this weekend and don't just want to just drink, smoke weed and watch WWE and binge watch "True Detective" again. Heck, you want to make "True Detective"!

Alright, you're not going to make "True Detective." But hell, you have an iPhone (dang, you dropped that in the toilet because you're too drunk). Okay, you still have that GoPro you got for Christmas. You haven't even opened the box yet. Why? You have nothing to shoot and the only thing you're opening is a can of beer.

Alright, you don't have to be drunk. You don't have to smoke weed. The real drug is your creativity. You want to make a short film. For fun. To see if you could do it. Because you and your buddies are creative, damn it. By the end of weekend, the beer cans have taken on strange shapes. The funny conversations are amazing and witty. These moments have to be harnessed for a short movie. The folks at Funny Or Die would love it. You're thinking, a stop motion film, where the beer cans are the characters and your friends supply the voices. If only you had story to place these cute beer can characters in. If only there was a book…

THE YOUTUBE NEW WAVE SHORT

TV is the new voice of cinema. Web episodes could the be the golden ticket to the TV world. Comedy Central's "Broad City" being a prime example. You're dying to ride this wave. You have an awesome TV/Web idea. You've had it for years. You have the whole season, characters, and situations scribbled down on napkins (or in your head). If only you had one episode written, you could start shooting it. If only there was a book…

THE FEATURETTE

Alright, you secretly want to make a feature film. But you want to make the short film first to illustrate how great the feature film will be. You read about "Napoleon Dynamite" and "Bottle Rocket" and you want to be the next Those Guys (if you haven't read about them, those films were once shorts). Your goal is perfectly fine. You just have to be honest with yourself. That's all this is about. You can create a fine short (that will eventually mature into this feature film). Now, if only there was a book…

… well, you get the idea.

PART II – DESIGNING YOUR SHORT

Okay, by now, you have a pretty good idea who the hell you are, what the hell you're making, and why the hell you're doing it.

I'm a Visionary who's making a Twilight Zone Short as a Drunk $5 Movie. I'm a Self-Muse, making a Autobio as a Summer Movie. I'm a Comic Genius making a Mock as a Film Student Film. In other words, you have the ingredients to make your lemonade. You've chosen your lemons, your water, your sweetener and any extras, like mint leaves and so on. You have the recipe. You have the container.

If your mind is cooking, I encourage you to start writing it before you even read this section. You may not even need this section. The idea is for you to write your short script. And if your mind is ready, YOU are ready.

Then, why is the second part here, you ask? Because I want to make sure you have NO excuses. Even if you're more certain of yourself now, you may run out of confidence later. This section is your training wheels. It's the portion of the cooking show where the chef practices the recipes.

That's right, I will now demonstrate how each of the "What The Hell Are You Making" shorts. I will also end each script with a magical tip. Let's write it!

MOMENT YOU'VE BEEN WAITING FOR

Drum roll please... trtrtrtrtrtrttrtrtrtrttrtrtrtrtr...

I was trying to think of banal, yet universal experience. So I did what many of us do when he can't come up with one, I asked my partner, Michelle Medvedoff (who coined the term "virtual fireplace") when I couldn't. She suggested, "why don't you just do it about getting shortchanged at the supermarket?"

Duh.

Yes, that is the perfect idea for many reasons. If we're honest with ourselves, we're just hunting and gathering food like every other animal on Earth (regardless of what we do); the supermarket experience is the height of this action. Therefore, shopping is a very primal experience. So is getting shortchanged. Money and food represent "survival."

I can see this "story" wrapping all six genres. I'm excited. My computer keys are recoiling in fear, knowing they're about to get battered by my fingers (and they should be).

Because I encourage weirdness (the title of this book is no accident), let's explore...

THE WEIRD MOVIE

SOUND: A clock ticking down, like a time bomb.

OPENING SHOT

CARTON OF EGGS. Yolk spills out of carton.

JUG OF MILK. Pools of white around bottle.

BABY SHOES. Just one. Burnt to a crisp like it was found on the side of the road.

REVEAL OUR LOCATION

WE ARE INSIDE A SUPERMARKET

These items - along with many following it - are on a conveyer belt.

THE WOMAN in line looks disoriented. And out of place.

She's well-dressed. Like she's going to a ball.

High heels. Cleavage.

There are many in line after her. Dressed commonly.

She looks around, sees CASHIERS in other lines. But CUSTOMERS wait behind THE WOMAN anyway.

WOMAN glances at her CASHIER. A young man of 16. Zits all over his face.

Deeply intimidated that he's standing before such a striking lady, he grins shyly.

> CLERK
> That will be 69 dollars and 69 cents please.

Reluctantly, WOMAN fishes out a bill. Coins and toiletry items spill out of her purse.

She hands the BILL to the CLERK.

Instead of a NAME TAG, the CLERK wears a little clock. These CLOSE HANDS are perpetually moving.

CLERK accepts the bill, hands her the CHANGE. Two fistfulls.

She looks in her hands and sees a bunch of EARTHWORMS. Crawling like Medusa's hair.

                    WOMAN
          This is not the correct change.

The CLERK raises his eye browse. Suggestively.

                    WOMAN
                (more succinctly)
          This is not the right change.

WOMAN looks at people in line. They all raise their eyebrows. Men and women alike.

Advancing towards her.

She steps back. Gazes at her groceries.

Spewing egg carton. Pooling milk bottle.

CLERKS at other AISLES also raise their eyebrows. And advance.

They're closing in.

She decides to RUN. In her high heels.

Not easy. Heels elongate like Pinocchio's nose.

3 inches become 4.

VEGETABLE SECTION

CLOCK seems to have grown in size, like something
you would see a train station.

She trudges through the vegetable section.
Everything is rotten.

Discolored carrots. Green sprouted potatoes.
Hole-filled lettuce. Sounds of flies buzzing.

She sees MOB of EYEBROWS RAISERS advancing, led
by the CASHIER.

She keeps running. Heels now FIVE INCHES.

CLACK-CLAK of HEELS echoing.

MEAT SECTION

Rotten meat everywhere. Sound of flies.

We can't tell what this meat is, except for the
UMBILICAL CORDS.

WOMAN sees she's SURROUNDED.

MOB coming from each side.

She realizes they're all holding out their hands.
All chanting:

                    MOB
        Tick tock, tick tock, tick tock…

In each hand are earthworms. WE HEAR SUCTION
NOISES from the WORMS.

WOMAN screams, horrified.

As CROWD envelops her.

WE HEAR sound of an alarm. Ear splitting.

The CROWD wraps the GIANT UMBILLICAL CORD and
MUMMIFY the woman. They WRAP UMBILLICAL CORD
until she's completely entombed inside it.

Until she's just a SHAPE of a woman, a
sarcophagus -- which they roll into the

BACKROOM

The rotten section. WE SEE there are many
sarcophagus.

THE END

DECONSTRUCTION

Weird, right? This movie made absolutely no sense. And yet, it told a story. You were engaged. You wanted to know what would happen next. And best of all, you want to see this short made, don't you? Admit it!

I wrote this short through the filter of the three W's; "Weird Movie" for a "Self-Muse" making her "Summer Movie."

The rules of "Weird Movie" are to free the unconscious. Most of the "bizarre stuff" such as the earthworms, the growing high heels, the umbilical cord materialized on the spot.

For example, as soon as the clerk handed the change to her, I told myself, if this was a dream, it would not be coins. Earthworms popped up. That's what I wrote.

I knew if I was writing for a "Self-Muse," it better be a juicy role. The Woman (The Self-Muse) has to be the object of desire. She needs opportunities to emit expressions. She's persecuted and wanted. She needs Musing opportunities. As many as I could provide.

And Summer Movie-wise? I realized while designing this short, I couldn't leave any stone unturned. The filmmaker I was writing for *needed* to make this film, *needed* to express powerful emotions bottled up inside for a long time.

"Won't I feel free writing *any* short scripts?" you might wonder. Not as free as this one. The Film Student Film, for example, has more rules. You're part of an institution. They have rules you must follow to make the grade or acquire the degree. Featurette may want to exemplify a character or two that we want to see more of. Same for the YouTube New Wave Pilot.

The real question is, aside from The Three W's, did I use other tricks to scribble this short this quickly and easily? Yes, of course.

There are *things* that live and breathe in stories - I'm going to say - most of the time. I don't believe in any concrete philosophy but you're likely just starting out and you need pillars. I will provide three pillars after each deconstruction. Then, I will show you how I used the pillar to my advantage.

The Forbidden Love

I know, I know, you've heard this a million times. Look, I'm not saying, boy meets girl, that kind of thing (though, I'm not limiting that either). I'm saying, one of the characters really wants something or someone, which is forbidden. In a movie. That's a Forbidden Love.

In our "Weird Movie" I simply had the cashier lust after the Woman. He raised his eyebrows. Then, everyone else did.

This "forbidden attraction" added a tension in the story that otherwise may not have existed. Imagine, Woman wanders in through the aisles with no one purusing her? Not as interesting, right?

Let's gauge some real movie examples (minus boy meets girl scenarios).

"Pee Wee's Big Adventure." Pee Wee loves his bike. It's taken from him. He chases it cross-country.

"The Piano." Holly Hunter loves her Piano. She's even willing to have sex to play her beloved keys.

"Terminator 2: Judgment Day." Edward Furlong loves his Terminator, even though Terminators will annihilate the world.

Someone wants someone or something…

… which they cannot have.

You don't have to revolve your story around this "wanting." Just have character to "want" what he can't have. The resulting tension can push the audience to a madness they can't get enough of (because we all want something we can't have in life).

Judd Appatow uses Forbidden Love so skillfully, he can write reams of dialogue and you'll keep watching. In "The 40 Year Old Virgin," Steve Carrell wants to get laid. In "Funny People," Adam Sandler wants Leslie Mann, even though she's married. In "This is 40", Paul Rudd and Leslie Mann want to love each other again, as they sink deeper into marital entropy. Dialogue Divas take notice. Employ "Forbidden Love" without shame and your characters can vomit words for a long time.

Let's proceed to the next one.

THE GENRE MOVIE

"THIS LINE IS CLOSED - PLEASE PROCEED TO NEXT LINE FOR SERVICE"-

This BAR is placed on the belt to ward off other customers.

The hand belongs to a man, wearing a suit.

CLOSE - CLEANING PRODUCTS

A sponge. Ajax. Laundry detergent. Six Pack of Guinness Beer. We are in a:

SUPERMARKET

WE SEE THE MAN buying this stuff.

Wears a suit like he just got off work.

He looks tired, but determined (based on his
purchases) to clean his place.

The WOMAN clearly notices him, her eyes widening
like she just saw something irregular.

By the time he turns back to her, she has looked
away. RINGING up each item robotically.

> WOMAN
>> Welcome to Albertson's, do you
>> have a club card?

> MAN
>> Sure.

MAN opens his wallet. There's tons of CARDS and
CASH. Extracts ALBERTSON'S CLUB CARD.

> WOMAN
>> Thanks, you'll save a lot.

She RINGS up his card and hands it back.
WE NOTICE she wears a WEDDING RING.

> MAN
>> Good, I'm in a saving mood.

Both of their BODY LANGUAGE is very flirtatious.
She is practically blushing from his presence.

> WOMAN

         I think you went over the limit.

She gesticulates to sign: "12 Items or less."

                    MAN
         Alright, remove one.

Suddenly, all the "chemistry" fades. The WOMAN
no longer smiles. No more flirting.

And he knows it.

                   WOMAN
         Why don't you remove it?

MAN recoils. Clears throat.

                    MAN
         I'm sorry. I'll make the decision.
         I won't put it on you.

He removes the AJAX.

                   WOMAN
         You sure you want to remove that?

MAN puts AJAX back.

                    MAN
         Should I... I mean...

MAN reaches in, takes out CLEANING GLOVES.
WOMAN notices he has a WEDDING RING too.

                         WOMAN
          That protects you from bacteria.
          And you want your hands clean, in case
          you caress your wife.

MAN puts CLEANING GLOVES back. Eyes SIX PACK
of GUINNESS. That's what he decides to remove.

The WOMAN smiles once more. She is impressed.

                         WOMAN
          Now, you have 12 items.

Relieved, MAN grins like a junkie.

                         MAN
          I want you to come back home. I'll do
          the cleaning and the cooking. See, I'm
          making dinner tonight.

                         WOMAN
          I don't care about that, Bill.

                         MAN
          I'll cut down the drinking.

NOW, the WOMAN smiles with relief.

                         MAN
          Today is our three year anniversary. I
          was going to go from bar to bar when
          I realized... that's the last thing
          I want.

WOMAN sees NEW ITEM rotating on the belt.

A bouquet of flowers.

                    WOMAN
               (on the verge of tears)
          That's not an item we sell.

                    MAN
          If I'm going over the limit, this is how
          I want to do it.

WOMAN takes BOUQUET, smells flowers, her eyes
welling up with tears.

                    WOMAN
          That'll be $28.46.

MAN hands her cash. She hands him change, but he
doesn't care -- he takes her hand, kisses it.

The change spills all over the floor.

                    MAN
          Will you come back, please?

Now, MAN is trembling in tears.

                    MAN
          I can't live without you.

                    WOMAN
          Neither can I.

```
MAN leaps over barriers and kisses his WIFE.
The kiss is so long, it goes beyond this film.

FADE OUT
```

DECONSTRUCTION

Genre was "drama." Through the prism of "Dialogue Diva" (you mean, you didn't notice all the chattering?) and "The Drunk $5 Movie." That's correct. The Drunk $5 movie.

The man and woman were the only two people in the store. The movie was one scene. I imagined the filmmaker worked at the store and had access to it after hours (not unlike Kevin Smith when he made "Clerks").

I limited the short to two characters and one event. I imagined a group of guys that get together one weekend, drink too much and perhaps realize that they had a little too much. The desire to channel their energies into more creative endeavors takes over them. They all have ambitions to have a girlfriend one day.

What is the Forbidden Love? In the beginning, it's the woman, in the end, it's the six pack of Guinness.

Yes, you can transcend the forbidden love, like in "The Piano." Holly Hunter is lovesick over her piano until the middle of the movie, when this emotion is transcended to Harvey Keitel – and she's a married woman, so it's, you know, forbidden.

Ready for the next pillar? Something that lives and breathes in a story most normal people can't see? No way you saw this coming. That's because it's...

The Secret Mystery

There's always a mystery. Always. I'm not saying, every movie is a mystery. I'm saying, there is always one. In a movie. Any movie. And I don't mean like "The Crying Game" (but I'm not excluding it either).

An actual mystery movie, like let's say "Gone Girl", is an overt mystery. The movie is telling you, hey, I'm a mystery, solve me. Did Ben Affleck murder his wife or not? But even in that movie, there was a secret mystery. Ben Affleck was cheating on his wife and you didn't know that until it was revealed.

Movies always have a "Secret Mystery." Take "Blue Jasmine." This film does not admit there is a mystery. Yet, there is indeed a mystery. There always is. You were not aware of it until its revelation . The filmmaker skillfully did not tell you and thus you didn't consciously investigate it.

At the end of "Blue Jasmine," Woody Allen reveals Cate Blanchett knew her husband was a crook all along. You didn't know that for the entire film. In fact, she's the one who turned him in. In the story, you considered her the naïve victim. Until the "Secret Mystery." She was not. We were the naïve audience.

At the end of "Fight Club," you find out Brad Pitt is a figment of Edward Norton's imagination (sorry if you haven't seen it... wait, you haven't seen "Fight Club"?)

Of course, there's the famous reveal at the end of "The Sixth Sense" where you find out Bruce Willis is a ghost (not sorry if you haven't seen "The Sixth Sense." You deserve that).

Let's throw in a comedy just for balance... "Planes, Train and Automobiles." At the end, we discover John Candy's wife is dead. She was never alive. Candy just talked about his spouse like she was still breathing. And yet "Planes" is a comedy. Now, imagine if you knew Candy was delusional about his wife in the beginning of the movie? Totally different movie, right?

What is the Secret Mystery rule? Hold something back from the audience (the more generic, the better) until a later time. It doesn't have to be "Sixth Sense"-like either.

"The Matrix." Cypher makes a deal with Agent Smith to have Morpheus captured. Secret mystery.

"Back To the Future." Michael J.Fox's mom is not a virgin. Secret Mystery.

"Reservoir Dogs." Tim Roth is the undercover cop. Yes, the guy who was bleeding to death most of the movie.

"Scarface." First time you saw it (I'm sure you've seen it fifty times like I have), you had no idea Tony's buddy, Manny, married his sister. Holy crap. At the worse time possible too. Tony is so shocked (and coked out), he empties his gun into his best friend.

"The Godfather, Part II" is the Mother of Secret Mysteries when Diane Keaton reveals she had an abortion. "An abortion, Michael!" Michael bans from her his family for life (or until "Godfather III").

"The Empire Strikes Back" is the Father of Secret Mysteries. Darth Vader was Luke Skywalker's pop all along! This revelation traumatized me when I was kid. Power of the Secret Mystery is sick.

Think of "The Secret Mystery" like your secret sauce. Well, you're making lemonade, so it's your secret sweetener or whatever. You get it. Pros always have one going. Sometimes, more than one.

Hold something back. Then gut punch the audience with it… or just slap them in the face. Or, I don't know, shake their hand with it. They will adore you for it. Why? Because life is full of secret mysteries!

What was the mystery in our Genre Film? You didn't know our MAN and WOMAN were married, did you? Admit it. You thought they were strangers. Well, they're not.

And what about our "Weird Movie," what was the Secret Mystery in that? Great thing about WM... *everything* is a mystery. Why does she have worms in her hands? Why are milk containers falling apart? Why do we hear clocks ticking so loudly? Best thing about "Secret Mystery"? You don't even have to resolve it. As long as it's there.

Tarantino never resolved *The Suitcase* in "Pulp Fiction." Chris Nolan never solved *The Spinning Totem* in "Inception." What about Stanley Kubrick's *monolith* in "2001: A Space Odyssey"? People are still debating what these *things* are.

That's the beauty of the The Secret Mystery. You don't even have to solve it. The best ones, people are still trying to solve long after they've seen the movie. Ready for the next one? Let's try...

THE MOCK

EXT. PARKING LOT - DAY

RALPHS SUPERMARKET marquee is CRUSHED. Imbedded in a giant CRATER like God's fist punched the ground. What happened?

                    MARINA (V.O.)
          It was my big break. But it's not
          my fault this happened.

INTERVIEW - HECTOR RUTHANLA

An overweight CAMERA MAN, who's well dressed and well lit for this interview.

                    HECTOR
        We approached it like any news story.

INTERVIEW - MARINA GOMES

Sits in darkness, small streaks of light sprawl her.

As if she doesn't want to look at anything bright.

                    MARINA
        I saw it as my big break.
        And I went after it.

EXT. PARKING LOT -- DAY

WE SEE MARINA's face for the first time. She is a gorgeous newscaster with too much make up.

In a hurry to get where she's going.

                    MARINA (V.O.)
        In this field, you don't think about how
        you could get hurt or how you could die.
        You think, story. Have to get it.

She looks thrilled, like she finally caught the "big one". That is, the "big story."

She catches her breath as she addresses camera.

                    MARINA
        Earlier today... outside of this
        Ralphs on Sepulveda and National, in
        West Los Angeles...

MARINA stops, nearly hyperventilates...

... as CAMERA pans to RALPHS SUPERMARKET... a
packed parking lot.

                    MARINA
        ... a very unusual shopping experience
        occurred inside this very supermarket.

CAMERA reveals a SMALL UFO parked amongst cars.

JUMP CUT

EXT. UFO - DAY

MARINA studies the UFO. Dirty and grimy.

She surveys the details with excitement, her
hands trembling.

CUT TO

INTERVIEW - MARINA GOMES

                    MARINA
        Thing looked like it hadn't been
        washed in a hundred years.

INTERVIEW - HECTOR

                         HECTOR
          It was a lot smaller than I thought.
          Size of a mini-van but circular.

INT. SUPERMARKET - PRODUCE AISLES - DAY

MARINA hurries past stunned customers.

                      MARINA (V.O.)
          Inside, no one could move.

Rows and rows of CATATONIC PEOPLE, many frozen in
the position they were in when they "saw it."

                      MARINA (V.O.)
          It reminded me of Pompeii, how they
          said people were just frozen into
          whatever they were doing when the
          volcano erupted.

Some clutch a box of cereal. Others hug a bag of
potatoes.

Others still grip their shopping carts tightly.

A BABYY BAWLS gutturally, secured in a car seat.

A FOUR YEAR OLD CHILD hides underneath the
lettuce section. Shaking like a leaf.

MARINA is trembling too, but out of excitement.
Gold fever in her eyes.

INT. DAIRY SECTION

The ALIEN is what you would expect. Four feet tall. Cone head. Buggy eyes. Stunned at the cheese section.

                    MARINA
          Excuse me, can I ask you a
          question...

When MARINA shoves the MIC in the ALIEN's face, the creature opens its mouth and BITES the MIC, lopping it off --

-- Leaving a stump with electrical wires sticking out. Chewing the instrument like it's something crunchy.

                    MARINA
          We need another Mic.

NOTICE, a shopping cart full of items. ALIEN is indeed shopping.

                    MARINA
          Holy shit. We have to...

ALIEN walks into the cleaning products aisle.

His SHOPPING CART follows, even though he is not physically pushing it - like he's using telekinesis.

                    MARINA

As you can see, our "visitor" is
shopping for food and accessories.
Perhaps this is a pit stop in his
journey to... wherever.

INT. SUPERMARKET - CHECK OUT AISLE

MARINA shoves a second MIC near ALIEN's face...
far enough that he can't eat it.

> MARINA
> Excuse me, sir. Is this a normal
> grocery shopping day for you?

Meanwhile, the CLERK is checking out the
groceries, too scared to do anything else.

There's a river of items on the belt. Looks
endless.

MARINA sees FOUR SHOPPING CARTS full of stuff.

> CLERK
> I can't keep ringing this stuff up,
> what am I going to do?

The TOTAL is now at 15,567.23 --

-- MARINA addresses the CAMERA.

> MARINA
> As you can see, that is one big
> grocery bill.

        (pivots to ALIEN)
     What do you plan to do with all this
     stuff, sir?

ALIEN doesn't reply. Hands CLERK a BRICK OF
HUNDREDS to pay for the groceries.

MARINA watches CLERK count change nervously.
ALIEN's hand remains there, waiting for his
change.

CLERK's hand vibrates uncontrollably as he hands
CHANGE to the three fingered ALIEN.

ALIEN stares at coins, puzzled.

At first, no reaction.

Then, his eyes gaze. Reptilian.

               MARINA
     Oh no. Oh Jesus.

FLOOR VIBRATES.

She loses balance. Groceries topple off belt.

CAMERA collapses.

Only thing standing still is ALIEN.

LIGHTS beam throughout the store.

GROCERIES levitate.

You could glimpse outside the window and see --

-- the STORE is defying gravity.

                    MARINA (V.O.)
          The extra terrestrial took the entire
          store.

                    HECTOR (V.O.)
          No one knows what happened after
          that.

MONTAGE - PEOPLE

Here, we will see people left in random parts of
the planet.

Each person looks exhausted, shocked and their
clothes are partially torn off.

- HECTOR finds himself in a landfill.

- CLERK walks with a blank look on the side of a
freeway.

- MARINA is in a corn field.

EXT. STREETS - DAY

MARINA walks, disoriented.

                    MARINA (V.O.)
          No one remembers what happened. But
          we were gone almost a year. All

```
        because the guy gave the alien the
        wrong change.

EXT. SUPERMARKET - DAY

A CRATER where the store once was. RALPHS
supermarket sign in pieces.

Skateboarders use it now.

FADE OUT
```

DECONSTRUCTION

It wasn't too original to have an alien in "The Mock", however if you're going to have extraterrestrials, this is the genre-du jour-for it.

This Mock was designed through the prisms of "The Featurette" (can't you just see the next two hours?) and "The Visionary." Original vision? Meteor crater in a supermarket parking lot. Not only does it spawn the entire story, it leads us to the third *thing* that lives like microbes in every story.

Once Upon A Time... or O.U.T. your story

OUT your movie with a STRONG OPENING. Look at any James Bond movie. Any film by Masters like Hitchcock, Orson Welles, orStanley Kubrick. They OUT their story.

"Good Fellas"... three guys are driving and there's something struggling in the trunk of their car.

"Annie Hall"... Woody Allen tells you his relationship just died.

"National Lampoon's Vacation"… a fun credit sequence with the family dog barking to the music.

I'm committed to these stories. Once Upon a Time What? Keep going. I want to hear more.

OUTing your story is very, very, very, very, very important. In the world of the short film, it could be what determines whether five people watch your film or 50,000. Why?

Because no one cares about you (with the exception of me). Why would they watch your short beyond one fraction of a second? I'll tell you why, because you will OUT your story.

Don't beat around the bush. You have five minutes beginning now. A great opening is a great opening. Beethoven's 5th Symphony is a cataclysmic opening, no matter what medium it is. We're still listening to it 200 years later.

OUTing does not have to be a Scorsese hammer blow. It could be like "Napoleon Dynamite" where credits are written on cafeteria plates. Music could set the mood ("Do The Right Thing"). Or dialogue ("Sex, Lies and Videotape"). Or a quote ("Hannah and Her Sisters"). Even a quote that is a lie ("Fargo" was not based on a true story, but guess how it opens?). Even a scroll ("Star Wars" and "Scarface") which is as *Once Upon a Time* as it gets…

If you were making a speech in a restaurant, this would be the part where you clink the spoon on a wine glass and shout "speech"! Imagine if you made your speech without the announcement? No one would hear you. And if anyone saw you, you would look crazy, talking to yourself.

This concludes *the three things in every story*. If you get stuck on your short, turn to these pillars. They help. A lot.

a) **The Forbidden Love.** Someone or something is lusted after.
b) **The Secret Mystery.** Leave a banal thing out until later.
c) **Once Upon a Time or OUT your story.** Open strong, baby.

Yes, we have three more pillars, but they will be in form of "considerations." As in things to consider rather than must-do's.

The *three things* I pointed out are not necessarily... must-dos but instead let's go with *strong encouragements*. Things I would tell myself if I had access to a time machine.

Ready for the fourth script?

THE AUTOBIO

OVER BLACK

SOUND of SQUEELING TIRES. REEEEeeeaaaaa.

EXT. SUPERMARKET - DAY

Parking lot, full. Every spot. Busy Saturday.

           MIKE (V.O.)
    It was the day of the big sale.
    Everything half off.

WE FOLLOW a CAR pulling into the PARKING LOT across the street --

-- THE OTHER SUPERMARKET

One with an empty lot.

                         MIKE (V.O.)
     You see there's stuff I value in life
     more than money.

WE SEE MIKE exit his car. A young man of 22 who
should get carded.

INT. SUPERMARKET - DAY

BEER SECTION. Guinness. Bud Light. Anchor Steam.
That's the one he's looking for.

                         MIKE (V.O.)
     Only day off. Needed to let off some
     steam. And I didn't want to wait in a
     line of 20 people to get it. I was
     buying time.

INT. SUPERMARKET - DAY

MIKE pushes a shopping cart. Only a six pack of
ANCHOR STEAM caged inside.

                         MIKE (V.O.)
     At least, that was the basic idea.

MIKE'S POV

He sees the IMPRESSION of a GORGEOUS WOMAN. The
CHECK OUT WOMAN. The closer he gets, the less
she's darkened.

The more she's enlightened. Beamed with sunlight like a holy object.

Her face, her body, jaw droppingly hot.

                    MIKE (V.O.)
          That's the first time I saw her.

WE SEE her name tag is upside down. He tilts his head to read it.

                    MIKE (V.O.)
          Her name tag was upside down, but I
          don't think she cared.

VANESSA chews gum and smokes a cigarette. The swirling heaps gives her a milky glow.

They talk, but we only hear what MIKE narrates.

                    MIKE (V.O.)
          I asked if she was bored. She
          shrugged. I asked her what a
          beautiful girl like her was doing
          working a place like this.

Her body language says: He's not getting anywhere. Finally, we hear her siren voice:

With lazy eyes and a "I could give a shit" demeanor, VANESSA is somehow even hotter.

>   VANESSA
> Going to college. Students loans
> will own my ass until I'm dead.

She exhales smoke.

>   MIKE
> What's your major?

>   VANESSA
> Anthropology. Or "My Apology" for
> wasting a good education.

>   MIKE (V.O.)
> I laughed. She didn't. She
> wasn't joking.

VANESSA hands his change. He looks at the coins.
Looks at the MANAGER. His NAME TAG is sideways.
OWEN.

>   MIKE (V.O.)
> She shortchanged me. But I didn't
> care. I went back again the next day.

INT. CHECK OUT - NIGHT

Again. Place is dead. No customers.

MIKE wears slightly nicer clothes. VANESSA is
not. There's one less button, revealing more of
her bosom.

OWEN observes from the same spot, his clothes filthier than yesterday.

He keeps his eyes on VANESSA mistrustfully. Something weird going on.

                 MIKE
    Where are you from, Vanessa?

VANESSA stares at her own bosom. WE SEE there's no name tag this time. She smiles thinly.

And briefly.

                VANESSA
    You know Columbus' three ships.
    Nina, Pinta and the whatever? I'm
    from the whatever.

              MIKE (V.O.)
    That was her way of telling me she
    was from "Santa Maria" on the central
    coast, next to where they turned water
    into wine - where the picture "Sideways"
    was filmed.

VANESSA hands him change. This time their fingers accidentally touch.

              MIKE (V.O.)
    Again, she shortchanged me. Again, I
    came back.

His eyes are radiated. He swallows nervously.

INT. CHECK OUT LINE - DAY

VANESSA's cleavage is even more visible. Three
buttons down now.

Her outfit is dirty like she hasn't taken it off
in a few days.

Her hair disheveled, her face sweaty. No AC in
here.

Even her cleavage is sweaty. MIKE is like a deer
in headlights.

He perspires through his nice clothes. His hair
is messed up from the heat and tension.

He is losing control over himself.

>   MIKE (V.O.)
> First time I went for beer, second
> time for potato chips, third time,
> thing I wanted wasn't for sale -- or
> was it?

VANESSA hands MIKE his change. He doesn't even
look. He's lost in her fierce eyes.

>   MIKE
> Made a lot of friends since
> you moved here?

>   VANESSA

Nope.

Her eyes prompt him to pay attention to his
change. He looks. Sees change and a RECEIPT.

> MIKE (V.O.)
> First time she gave me a receipt.

MIKE is terrified. Turns to OWEN, who's glaring
at him. Yet, MIKE never moves.

Then, femme fatale's voice lures him back.

> VANESSA
> But I'm always ready to make friends.
> Know anyone?

MIKE can hardly look at her. So much heat and
smoke, her clothes are nearly transparent.

INT. MIKE'S CAR - LATER

MIKE checks the receipt. Doesn't show the totals.
There's a message.

"IF OWEN GOES, WE CAN BE TOGETHER"

> MIKE (V.O.)
> That villain had her trapped inside. I
> had to free her.

MIKE's hand trembles. He lights up cigarette. He
can't see clearly into THE SUPERMARKET...

... but it appears like OWEN is grabbing his
VANESSA against her will.

                    MIKE (V.O.)
          She wanted freedom so she could be with
          me. Since that six pack of Anchor Steam,
          I knew there was something between us.
          That's what she meant when she said
          "know anyone?"

INT. CHECK OUT LINE - VERY LATE NIGHT

MIKE buys FIREWOOD, like the six pack he bought
in the first scene, but much bigger.

                    MIKE
          Vanessa, I know someone who wants to
          be your friend. Me.

VANESSA looks different tonight. Buttoned up.
Pristine. Hair combed. Even name tagged. Yes,
she WEARS the nametag. VANESSA emblazoned on her.

                    VANESSA
          Sure.

                    MIKE (V.O.)
          I noticed for the first time Owen was
          not there.

No on else there except for both of them. In the
entire store.

                    VANESSA

I'm glad you said that, Michael. I'd be
too shy to assume I'm anyone's friend.

VANESSA hands him change, but this time, when he
reaches for it, she pulls him toward her. They
KISS.

Their lips connect intensely. MIKE's eyes search
the empty aisles of the store.

No one is looking.

Except OWEN who appears from the canned goods
section.

                    OWEN
          What do you think you're doing,
          Vanessa?

When she lets him go, she's out of breath. Her
bosom moving up and down vulnerably.

                    MIKE (V.O.)
          There was the villain who had my
          woman trapped like a glass jar. I
          would free her.

MIKE rips out one of the WOODEN LOGS and batters
OWEN with it -- until he's a bloody mess.

                    MIKE (V.O.)
          I would take Vanessa with me back to the
          two bedroom I shared with two others.

But I wouldn't share her. She would
be mine. All --

OWEN is done. Barely alive. His last words are...

                    OWEN
      Kissing customers is against store
      policy.

He dies.

                    MIKE (V.O.)
      Weird thing to say as last dying
      words. It was enough for my
      instincts to know, I was done for.

OWEN notices VANESSA's name tag reflect something
bright - before he can figure it out, he is
bathed in police lights.

Which illuminate VANESSA, full of tears and
terror in her eyes.

She's not the same woman who asked him to kill.
She's now a victim.

                    MIKE (V.O.)
      When I saw her face, I put two and
      two together too late.

COPS drag MIKE away. VANESSA cries, comforted by
OTHER COPS.

MIKE has a blank look.

INT. INTEROGATON ROOM - NIGHT

TWO COPS question MIKE, who's traumatized from
heartbreak.

                COP
     You murdered the manager? You raped
     the employee? And you emptied the
     safe? Admit it or get the chair.

TIGHT SHOT -- THE STORE SAFE

An empty safe. All gone.

INT. VANESSA'S CAR - DAY

She wears sunglasses. And nonchallance. She
shoves "VANESSA" name tag into glove compartment
-- where piles of other name tags reside.

            MIKE (V.O.)
     She stole 85 grand in cash and needed
     a fall guy. I didn't care about
     that. It was the other thing she
     stole that crushed me. My heart.

EXT. HIGHWAY - DAY

VANESSA flies by a parking lot full of cars.

            MIKE (V.O.)

```
If you want to avoid her, go to the
place that has a sale... or risk
being part of her "My Apology" Degree.
 (beat)
Unless, she changed her major.
```

FADE OUT

DECONSTRUCTION

This Autobio is based on the night I met my girlfriend. At a movie theatre called the NuWilshire. She was worked at the snack bar. I was there to interview a producer for a Canadian guy's documentary.

I was struck by her. We talked. Had a nice conversation, which led to a phone number exchange. What's autobiographical in the short?

I did ask her if she was bored. She did not have a name tag. She is from Santa Maria. She did go to UCLA for an Anthropology Degree. I did ask her if she had made a lot of friends since moving here. And she is really hot. The rest is made up.

I did not go to prison. She did not rip off her employer. And I didn't kill anyone, nor was I 22 when I met her (I was 29). But there is truth in the emotion of the story – and that is what you are seeking in an Autobio. Truth in the emotion.

I can write my girlfriend as a Femme Fatale because I do think she can have that kind of power over dudes if she wants to, but not because she's a beautiful, manipulative man-eater. In reality, she's just beautiful, but very down-to-Earth and low maintenance (and, lucky me, not interested in man-eating). There is only truth in how I amplified the story.

The Autobio does not even have to be your experience. It just has to be based on something real. The late Wes Craven based "A Nightmare on Elm Street" on a real event. A group of Cambodian refugees were dying in their nightmares. Craven was inspired, put himself in the minds of the Cambodian and even named one our greatest villains after his high school bully, Fred Krueger.

Although "Scarface" was a remake, Oliver Stone entered the Cuban underworld in Miami and met with real life coke dealers; Cubans who got rich really fast but got killed really fast. The classic film has an unmistakable authenticity.

Spike Lee based "Do The Right Thing" on the Howard Beach Incident.

Matt Groening based "The Simpsons" on his family, even naming the characters after his siblings.

John Hughes wrote "Vacation" based on his father's crazy real life antics during their road trips.

And guess what Paul Fieg based "Freaks and Geeks" on? Going to high school with his older sister.

Finally, David Lynch was so obsessed with the O.J. Simpson murder trial, he made "Lost Highway" about a man who may or may not have murdered his blonde wife.

The rose bush of authenticity is everywhere. Pluck from it freely. Anything you want. Any real life experience can be a short film.

What other prisms did I use? Film School Film and The Dry Comic Genius. The Noir Elements were played for laughs, but not everyone will get it, therefore it's dry. Plus, this short is heavily coated with a technique I did not use in the other shorts. This is my first "consideration."

To Narrate or Not to Narrate...

In feature screenwriting, Narration is a taboo. A huge no-no. A deadly sin. Having the protagonist or a third person narrate your story is the first thing they teach you NOT to do in screenwriting class.

Regardless, some really good films are filled with voice over, such as "Barry Lyndon," "Dogville" and "Casino." Check out the noir classic, "Detour" (last I checked, available on YouTube, incredible movie) or one of the very first microbudget films "Boxes" directed by Rene Besson in 2000. "The Noah," made in 1975 by Daniel Bourla, is about the last man on a desert island, after a nuclear war wiped everything out. The whole movie, you hear this poor guy arguing with himself in his head.

Frowned upon in features, but in the world of shorts, narration is encouraged. Alexander Payne's short from "Paris, Je T'aime" is one of the funniest shorts I've ever seen. All in voice over. Nick Offerman's "The Gunfighter" employs brilliant use of voice over. Characters argue with the invisible narrator, who predicts every character's death.

Using narration, of course, depends on who the hell you are. For a Comic Genius like Offerman, it works wonders. However, a Dialogue Diva may prefer to toy with the dialogue, as that is her strength.

In my narration, I used a Film Noir texture, partially to show how delusional the protagonist was. The narration insulated the viewer in narrow point of view to create tension.

Ready for the Fifth What The Hell Are you Making?

THE TWILIGHT ZONE SHORT

CLOSE - SIGN "EXPRESS LANE"

Sign looms with doom. "107 Items or less."

> MAN (V.O.)
> At last, I got in the express line.

CLOSE - HANDS CLENCHING

Shopping cart. Sound of cage rattling.

> MAN (V.O.)
> I know I have things in order now.
> Not like last time.

CLOSE - MONEY CRUMPLED

In palm of his hand.

CLOSE - WHEELS

Twirling resistantly. Hasn't been oiled in a while. Reeeeaaahh.

> MAN (V.O.)
> Nothing can take my confidence away.

CLOSE - EYES

Agape. Sweat pouring. METAL KLANGING.

> MAN (V.O.)

I will be free of this place.

ON SHOPPING CART

Filled to the brim with products. Cereal. Milk.
Toilet paper. Vegetables. Meat.

                    MAN (V.O.)
          I have completed my list.

CLOSE - EYES

Blinking from sweat. And from what he sees.

                    MAN (V.O.)
             Nothing will tempt me.

POV - WHAT HE SEES

Candy bar displays tease. Snickers. M & M's.
Avenues of sweets, even Toblerones.

                    MAN (V.O.)
             Certainly not that poison.

CLOSE - FACE

Exhausted, raw-nerved, like they're being fed
into a dungeon. You can hear many WHEELS
SCREECHING.

CLOSE - WHAT HE SEES

Candy bars are even more delicious looking. 70%
dark chocolate. Truffles.

> MAN (V.O.)
> Oh no, I love 70% dark. I do have
> room for one or two more items.

His hand reaches for one. Then two.

MEDIUM SHOT

Reveals MAN is behind FOUR CUSTOMERS, each with
carts filled to the brim.

The one CUSTOMER before him is a NERVOUS WOMAN
being reprimanded.

> CLERK
> Too many items! This is the 107
> items or less line!

NERVOUS WOMAN is escorted to the back of the
line. OLD MAN behind her is next. He's trembling.

CLOSE - WHAT HE SEES

More temptations. Potato chips. His favorite.
Timothy's Sea Salt and Vinegar. He snag two
packs.

                          MAN (V.O.)
          Oh, I love those chips. I have
          room for a little more.

He tosses the packs in the SHOPPING CART.

WIDER SHOT

Reveals MANY, MANY customers behind him. The
queue is so long, we're not sure where it ends.

They look very tired, like they crossed a desert
to get here.

OUR MAN

He is now NEXT in line. His face, nervous yet
prepared.

He sees OLD MAN before him being addressed by the
CLERK.

                          CUSTOMER
          You have the appropriate items.
          You may leave.

This OLD MAN is trembling and even weeping.

                          MAN'S VOICE
          Old Man Henry... he's tried to get
          out forever. Good for him.

The door parts open, revealing a BRIGHTNESS so
intense, you only see the OLD MAN's SILLHOUETTE
as he leaves for good.

                    SECURITY GUARD
          Place each item properly!

CLOSE - CONVEYOR BELT

MAN uses two hands to place the ITEMS carefully,
like they're valuables. WE SEE he trembles more
than the old man.

CLOSE - MAN'S FACE

His eyes, dilating with tension.

CLOSE - GROCERIES

Toilet paper. Paper towels. Mustards. Pickles.
It's endless.

The cacophony of beep--bee--beep is like a pulse.

CLOSE - CLERK

Although he's ringing item after item, his eyes
remain on the CUSTOMER. Boring into him with deep
judgment.

CLOSE - MAN'S FACE

Grinning with vanishing confidence.

As the beep-beep-beeps slow down.

And then, they stop.

CLOSE - MAN'S FACE

Awaits verdict.

> MAN (V.O.)
>> (hopeful)
>> Under 107 items?

CLOSE - CLERK'S FACE

Hateful.

> CLERK
>> Your total is $69.55.

CLOSE - MAN'S HANDS

Cups money to CLERK.

CLOSE - CLERK

Disgusted.

> CLERK
>> Can't you read. Says exact change!
>> Back of the line!

CLOSE - MAN

Pleading, begging.

                         MAN
          No, no, please, I have, I have...

But SECURITY GUARDS are already dragging him
away. MAN's SHOES scrape the floor.

WIDE SHOT

Reveals there must be HUNDREDs of people in this
line. Orchestra rusty shopping cart wheels.

MAN AND SECURITY GUARDS

Meanwhile, our MAN begs to finish his
transaction. As he is dragged. He is tossed on
the floor. His body SLAPS pavement.

                         MAN
          I had under 107 items. I had...

                    SECURITY GUARD
             You didn't have correct change. Back
             of the line.

BACK OF THE LINE

Our customer sobs, teetering, holding his cart
for balance.

                         MAN
             But, it took me two years to get to
             the check out. Last time I was in
             Express, it was 105 Items or less.

> SECURITY GUARD
Next time, make sure you have exact
change.

> MAN
Last time I had exact change but
I was one item over...

SECURITY GUARDS don't care. They stomp away like
jack boots.

The MAN is last in a line that outstretches a
quarter mile.

DEVASTASTED CUSTOMERS in front of him offer
pitying looks.

> MAN
> (defeated)
... now, I had 107 items but didn't
have the correct change.

THE WOMAN before him looks wrecked and hopeless.

> WOMAN
You want my change?

> MAN
Sure.

> WOMAN
Of course, your total won't be the
same next time.

> MAN
>
> Yes, it will. It will be the same.
> 107 items at $69.55 cents. You
> watch. You watch. Even if it takes
> me ten years to get there.

His voice echoes throughout the high ceilings
like even his sound will never escape.

As WE EXPAND across the STORE which has aisle
after after aisle after aisle... so many, it
would take a math genius to count.

> MAN'S VOICE
>
> I will get in the express line again.
> I will not be tempted. I will check out
> one day. I will.

FADE OUT

DECONSTRUCTION

Twilight Zone Short. Next Scorsese. Film Student Film. You may wonder what the difference is between Twilight Zone and Weird Movie. They both can be "weird", but they are different animals.

Twilight Zone makes rational sense within the world. The "weirdness rules" are set up in the beginning and must be followed to maintain the Twilight Zone essence.

We know he needs 107 items to get out. Any Secret Mystery that may materialize, such as needing perfect change, is within the logic of the set-up. The coins won't be bigger. There won't be unicorns galloping in the store. There won't be an earthquake.

Any new challenge occurs for a reason, in this case, to keep him trapped in the store.

Whereas a Weird Movie is more plastic. If you recall, our WM had worms instead of coins, her high heels kept growing, giant umbilical cord… these images had no explanation. No overtly reasonable ones, anyway. Its style is "unconscious."

Twilight Zone Movie is making more of a social statement, in this case about how the shopping experience can be hell. It is very "conscious." Even down to the sounds, which brings us to our second "consideration."

Sound your picture

A film is sound AND picture. That's very easy to forget when you're told you're writing for a visual medium.

Now, you may not care about sound. You might have a soundtrack prepared that will flow underneath your masterpiece. Movies have been made with horrible to no sound at times (and even done well, especially in the silent era, but still…).

I'm just here to tell you that sound *does* exist. The yin to the visual's yang. Sound is a great instrument when used in a screenplay, to visualize what you envision – and to communicate it to others.

A great film is a perfect symmetry of two senses, seeing and hearing. Discarding what is heard without weighing if you need it could be something you will regret.

Go on any professional film set. They check the sound religiously. If the sound isn't good, they will do a take over again. I'm prepared to say that sound is MORE important than picture.

Why? We're all different in how we color our visuals. Some of you may describe what a character wears, others may write paragraphs about furniture, while others still may specify a car in detail. Nothing wrong with any of them. You specify what's important to you.

Point is: you will pay proper attention to the visual no matter what. But sound, that's the thing you don't see. And it can be just as powerful. Close your eyes and imagine what your story sounds like. Then write it down.

David Lynch spent years sound designing "Eraserhead." Today, he has a sound mixing room in his house (I know, I've been in his house). Re-watch any of Lynch's films and examine why he is so unique. It's his sound design. Victorian London in "Elephant Man," beneath the perfect lawns of suburbia in "Blue Velvet," or even the crazy antics of his odd TV show, "On The Air"... the sound is always king. It goes inside you as his stories unfold.

Think about this. A good portion of your script will likely be sound, since dialogue is sound. Why limit the use of sound to just what people say?

Consider your character's environment; perhaps, they work in a steel mill ("Deer Hunter"), perhaps they are surrounded by threatening city sounds ("Punch Drunk Love"), or your protagonist is being chased by a vicious truck ("Duel"... Spielberg employed lion sounds for the rig).

In our Twilight Zone Short, we used the sounds of rusty shopping cart wheels, the security guard's shoes, and so on to create a dungeon like atmosphere. The sound was half the story.

Check out Joseph Bennett's short "Odin's Afterbirth." Witness excellent use of sound in this dark, twisted, revenge fantasy. The wetness of the blood, the slicing of flesh, the metallic ringing of the Medieval weapons. It becomes 3-D in your mind.

Ready for the last script? Are you sad? You're going to miss me? Aww, don't worry. If you get heartsick, you can re-read the book. It was re-written for that purpose. Review it till you're sick of me.

For "The Spoof," I toyed with different possibilities. I considered doing a "Good Fellas" spoof where mob guys worked in a health food supermarket. I also leaned on doing a "Taken" spoof, where a man's dog is kidnapped and taken to a supermarket butcher (the canine will be sold as meat if he doesn't get there on time).

But one of the objectives to "The Spoof" is to utilize a recent film, a movie that is in the zeitgeist, something "Saturday Night Live" or "South Park" would make fun of. The last good film I saw was the Pixar movie, "Inside Out." A G-Rated Film. WARNING: This version is not G-Rated.

THE SPOOF

INT. CONTROL ROOM - NIGHT

KNOCK on the door. A healthy woman approaches, wears exercise clothes. Her voice, cheerful and upbeat.

>   HEALTHY WOMAN
>   Who is it?

>   KIND VOICE
>   Delivering the day's shopping list.

HEALTHY WOMAN opens the door -- and immediately is SHOT -- FIRED repeatedly -- by a gun --

>   HEALTHY WOMAN
>   AAaaaghhh...

The WOMAN falls on the ground bleeding as THREE SKI MASKED HOODLUMS enter the premises.

And they keep firing --

-- BLASTING a WELL FIT MUSCULAR MAN, who collapses.

-- a YOUNG MAN who WEARS GLASSES.

-- there is A MIDDLE AGED SMOKER, who doesn't even bothering moving, like he wants to die.

They don't shoot him.

Three masked HOODLUMS are... well, they'll
introduce themselves.

First guy removes his mask. There's tumors all
over his neck.

                    CANCER
         Nice to meet you, I'm Cancer.

CANCER shakes hands with SMOKER, who introduces
himself:

                 RATIONALIZATION
         What's up, I'm Rationalization.

HEART DISEASE removes her mask. An emaciated
woman with a smoker's voice.

                  HEART DISEASE
         Great to meet you, I'm Heart Disease.
         That's diabetes.

DIABETES is a fat man, constantly limping and
eating candy bars. Eyes, bloodshot.

                    CANCER
              (to RATIONALIZATION)
         Oh man, I've heard a lot about you.
         Your ability to make anything sound
         good, we need that.

                        RATIONALIZATION
          Well, things are good.

                           CANCER
             Yes, yes, they are.

HEART DISEASE gesticulates above.

                        HEART DISEASE
          Look, look, he's inside.

They SEE a SCREEN showing the POINT OF VIEW of
someone in a SUPERMARKET -- pushing a SHOPPING
CART.

WE SEE tons of vegetables -- onions, spinach,
lettuce.

                          DIABETES
          Gross.

                        RATIONALIZATION
          Well, they are colorful.

CANCER moves up to the CONSOLE -- which controls
the MIND of the PERSON on the screen. As WE CUT
TO:

INT. SUPERMARKET -- DAY

JOE is a fit man in his mid-forties. His cart is
hall full of vegetables. Constantly checks
shopping list he scribbled with his wife.

                        JOE
     They are colorful.

ON SHOPPING LIST

Lettuce, tomatoes, spinach, broccoli, beets...

... when his CELL PHONE goes off. He answers.

ON JOE

Talking on the phone.

                    VOICE OF WIFE
     Joe, I forgot, can you pick up some
     zucchini. I have tasty vegan dish I
     want to try tonight.

                        JOE
     Sure sweety.

He hangs up the phone, but suddenly his face
changes. The man starts mimicking his own p-
whipped voice.

                        JOE
     Sure sweety. Whatever you want, sweetie.
     Ugh. What's wrong with you? I'm the one
     shopping. I'll get what I want.

INT. MIND CONSOLE ROOM - CONTINUOUS

CANCER is ecstatic. Moving the levers expertly
like a deejay.

                    HEART DISEASE
          Yeah, where's the real stuff?

In the background, BLEEDING MUSCULAR MAN protests
with fading strength.

                    MUSCULAR MAN
          You'll never... get away... with
          this?

                       DIABETES
          Shut up.

DIABETES kicks the bleeding man.

                    HEART DISEASE
          Ha, ha. Look, look.

THE SCREEN

Shows the POTATO CHIPS AISLE. HEART DISEASE,
DIABETES and CANCER jump up and down, thrilled.

                    RATIONALIZATION
          Potatoes. That's a vegetable.

                    HEART DISEASE
                     (thrilled)
          Yes, yes, potatoes are a vegetable.

HEART DISEASE rushes to the CONSOLE. CANCER is
only too happy to let her take over.

INT. POTATO CHIP SECTION -- CONTINUOUS

JOE snags one bag, then two bags of POTATO CHIPS.
Drone-like, he says:

> JOE
> Potato is a vegetable.
> Good for you.

JOE grabs two more BAGS. Then THREE BAGS. As WE

CUT TO:

INT. CONSOLE

This time, DIABETES is in control. She is
practically salivating.

> DIABETES
> Oh Jesus. Look at that.

THE SCREEN

Shows the candy aisle. Avenues of CHOCOLATE CANDY
BARS.

> RATIONALIZATION (V.O.)
> Dark chocolate has less sugar.

INT. CANDY SECTION

JOE grabs piles of CHOCOLATE CANDY BARS and even unwraps one right there in the store. And begins eating it.

> JOE
> Mmmh, it's been so long. That is so good. Plus, dark chocolate has less sugar.

INT. MIND CONSOLE ROOM

CANCER is now in control again, where he is giddy from excitement.

> CANCER
> Oh yes, baby, come to poppa.

THE SCREEN

Shows the meat section. JOE grabs --

-- DELI TURKEY MEAT.

> RATIONALIZATION (V.O.)
> White meat is good for you.

-- GROUND BEEF -- 33% from China, 33% from Tennessee, 33% from Ireland.

> RATIONALIZATION (V.O.)
> Ireland has very fresh red meat.

-- SAUSAGES.

                    CANCER (V.O.)
         I love sausages. I don't need a
         reason.

INT. SUPERMARKET

JOE tosses PACKAGE of ITALIAN SAUSAGES in
shopping cart.

                    JOE
         I don't need any reason to eat one of
         my favorite foods. I love sausages.

INT. MIND CONSOLE

HEART DISEASE is now in control. He looks crazed.

                    HEART DISEASE
         So much salt. Yes, yes.

INT. CHECK OUT LINE - LATER

As JOE leaves, his shopping cart is full of
POTATO CHIPS, COOKIES, MEATS, CANDY, CHOCOLATE,
COCA-COLA, BEER.

Cell phone is ringing, but JOE doesn't care.

                    JOE
         It's just that nagging bitch. Wants
         me to bring home a garden. Fuck
         that. I came here through my own
         force. I'm getting what I want.

The CLERK is uncomfortable hearing this, but he has to stay professional.

> CLERK (O.S.)
> You forgot your change, sir.

INT. MIND CONSOLE ROOM

CANCER, HEART DISEASE and DIABETES stab and shoot the three victims they attacked until they're pretty much dead.

> HEART DISEASE
> I will own his heart.

> DIABETES
> I will own his blood.

> CANCER
> I will own his colon.

All three laugh maniacally.

INT. JOE'S CAR -- NIGHT

He's eating chips, cookies and drinking a beer while flashing police lights illuminate around him. POLICE MAN's VOICE is heard off screen.

> POLICE MAN
> Have you been drinking sir?

                    JOE
     I've been doing what the hell I want.
     That's what I've been doing.

INT. APARTMENT - NIGHT

JOE's very healthy WIFE, SAMANTHA is doing yoga
in front of the TV when the phone rings.

She stops to pick the phone and to her horror,
she hears a drunk, mean voice of:

                    JOE
     You controlling bitch. This is my only
     phone call. Come and get me.

TO BE CONTINUED

DECONSTRUCTION

Why "To Be Continued"? This "Inside Out Spoof" was written as
a You Tube New Wave Short, in the guise of "The Comic Genius,"
plus a minor in "The Pragmatic."

I imagined a webisode where a man fights his cravings to stay
healthy, spoofing the characters from "Inside Out", as Comic
Genius generally do.

Pragmatic-wise, you might have noticed, many of the shots in
the supermarket are POV or JOE shopping alone. When you hear
the CLERK, his voice is off screen (you can add that sound later).

While I suggest getting permission to shoot in a location like a
supermarket, you can always steal a location with the cameras we
have today (please don't use your only phone call on me). I still

say, get permission. You'd be surprised how easy it is (but if you have to steal your location, I won't judge you).

Now, for the last "consideration."

Go Theme-less At Your Own Risk

You don't have to have a "theme." But screenwriting is so much easier when you have one.

Life. Is. Sooooo. Much. Easier. Every great screenwriting book (Blake Snyder's "Save The Cat" and Mark Evan Schwartz "On Writing: A Screenplay") insists you need one. Stephen King strongly suggests having a "theme" in his book "On Writing." Beethoven has a theme for each of his great symphonies (hell, I don't think you can write a symphony without one). What is the theme?

In feature length screenwriting, the theme is a question which is debated by the story until the very end.

For example, in "When Harry Met Sally..." it's "can men and women be friends"? In "Lethal Weapon" it's, "do you have to be crazy to be a cop?" In "Bullets Over The Broadway," it's, "are artists above morality?" In each of these films, the question is answered. Men and women cannot be friends. You don't have to crazy to be a cop (but it's close). Artists are above morality. You may not agree, but that's how those films concluded their themes.

Think about the last story you told. You explained how you were driving and someone cut you off. Why would he do that? What's the guy's problem? What did I do to him? Stories are questions which are debated... thematically.

Does the same rule apply for short screenplays? Sort of. A theme is always the DNA of a story. Whether you see it or not, it is there. Not just in films, but any story... a news story, even a commercial, even a theme park has a theme.

I took an architectural tour of downtown Los Angeles recently and discovered that buildings have themes. The Water and Power building had these Greek Gods icons, one representing water, the other power. Some buildings had an Eagle, which represented wisdom. Every single foundation had a theme that shaped it. You may never see it, but their DNA influenced the entire skyscraping structure.

Here's an easy way to think about "theme." There is something you complain about everyday (I know there is for me). The weather, the government, the opposite sex, your children, your parents, your siblings, you spouse, your pet, your phone company, your church… something pisses you off. Think of your theme as concerns dear to your heart. Your body of work as a filmmaker will likely contain only themes that you will revisit, over and over again.

John Woo ("The Killer", "Hard Boiled") makes films about "the price of friendship."

Quentin Tarantino ("Pulp Fiction," "Kill Bill") makes films about "the unstoppable cycle of revenge."

Catherine Breillat ("Fat Girl," "Romance") makes films about the "fear of a woman's body."

Douglas Sirk ("All That Heaven Allows," "Imitation of Life") made films about "the compromise of fitting in."

Wes Anderson ("The Royal Tenembaums," "Rushmore") makes films about "nostalgia" and "the inability to grow up."

Alfred Hitchcock ("The Birds," "Psycho") made films about "guilt" and "the fear of getting caught."

Lina Whurtmuller ("Seven Beauties" and "Swept Away") makes films about "the battle of sexes."

That is how these filmmakers complain about society, culture, the government, the opposite sex, etc. Think of any body of work. There's only a limited amount of themes a filmmaker works with.

No director makes films about 50 themes. There's usually several, at the most. James Cameron only has one theme. "The sin of technology." All of his films are about that. "Aliens," "The Terminator," "Titanic," "Avatar." Technology is what Cameron wants to talk about, and don't think Jim is not aware of it. Seasoned storytellers usually are aware, because they've been doing it a long time. Novice storytellers are usually not aware, since they're just discovering what they want to say.

"Raging Bull" is about loneliness. The opening image is a Robert DeNiro, shadow boxing by himself in an empty, as smoke heaps like a fog. Directly influenced by the theme. He's a man who would fight even if there was no one there. He's alone, because no one wants to be with him. The last image is DeNiro talking to himself in front of the mirror. Are we our worse enemies?

"Rocky" opens with a slow pan from the top of a crumbling gym, that descends to the bottom, where two men are beating hell out of each other. It's described in Stallone's screenplay as a giant garbage can. This is the theme. Once your life hits bottom, is that it? You see how knowing your theme helps the design of your movie?

Even a very strange film like "Eraserhead" is fueled by an underlying theme... about fatherhood. Maybe Lynch himself did not know what theme was, but understood being a father had something to do with it. The sound and images are directly influenced by the "fatherhood" question. Dinner with in-laws, baby that won't stop crying, etc.

So, you ask again, does the same rule apply for short screenplays? No, it doesn't. It would help you tremendously.

Unlike a feature screenplay, you do not need a thematic question. A half-assed theme will do. A short statement or a single word will shape your vision. My film is about "death," "taxes," "overprotective parents," "the crap people put in their bodies," "why people love sports," "slavery to the internet" and so on and so forth.

A film is a story told in symbols. These symbols can be written any you want in your laptop. However, when you shoot it, you need these symbols *for real*. If you wrote in a TANK, you're going to need to find a real tank or CGI one. It helps if you knew ahead of time that this tank did not fit your theme?

In the editing room, you may even wind up cutting the tank out, realizing you didn't need this goddamn thing that costs you huge favors, and damaged half your neighborhood. Or you may leave the monstrosity in, because it was so difficult to acquire. And thus, hurt your story.

What's important is to uncover your half-assed theme while it's still on paper. Stephen King has discussed finding hi book's themes after writing the first draft. The discovery of his theme helped him shape his second draft and complete his book.

Once more, I strongly caution against NOT having a theme. Yes, good films have been done without the awareness of a theme. If you have money and resources to burn, and you feel like knowing too much will hurt your creative process, by all means, don't be aware of your theme.

If money and time is not the issue, if you're shooting episodes of two roommates in an apartment and you're not sure what the theme is, by all means, keep going. I just know that your life would be easier if you eventually discovered the theme. The comedy about two roommates in the apartment will sharpen and you will understand why you want to tell this story.

Some people are intuitive storytellers. That may be you. Even if you are, I strongly warn you about NOT using a theme. Films are visual, and even though they're a lot cheaper to make than they used to be, it still takes work to find the right location, or clothe an actor, or a particular car, etc. Even if you're making your film for $5, productions headaches still transpire.

Did I use a theme in the Six What the Hell Am I Making? Of course.

Weird Movie. Biological clock is ticking. Once I told my brain this was the theme, images popped up, like overflowing egg cartons and earthworms which made sense to the story in a deeper way.

Genre Movie. Can a Husband clean up his life? That's why he was buying cleaning products, then gave up the six pack. Ouch.

The Mock. Is Ambition Dangerous? An alien everyone is terrified of can only be approached by a news woman.

Autobio. Men see Women as victims, but are they? You see where that led the protagonist.

Twilight Zone Movie. When did shopping become so difficult?

The Spoof. One word: Control. Joe feels he is controlled by his wife. He didn't just blow up that second. Eventually, he is controlled by the diseases fighting for his body.

Every one of these shorts was created with a theme or a half-assed theme. Once you understand what you want to say, your fingers can do a lot of work on the keyboard, because your creative mind will be enslaved to your theme. You'll be amazed.

THE RECIPE

Let's recap our Lemonade Recipe.

1. You know who the hell you are.
2. You know what the hell you're making.
3. You know why the hell you're making this.

In your story, you must have:

4. A strong opening.
5. A Forbidden Love.
6. A Secret Mystery (if your genre is Mystery, then its no secret)

You will consider using:
7. A half-assed theme.
8. Narration.
9. Sound with your picture.

You have all the ingredients to make lemonade: lemons, water, your secret ingredient, a vessel to pour in. Wow. You are more ready now than you were when you started this book.

Your story should be pretty sharpened in your mind. You should be excited, because you're about to write your first short screenplay (then shoot it, since you'll be so thrilled at how well it turned out). Should you hire a writer, you will understand how to communicate your vision succinctly, so that you'll get the script you want.

The short film medium will only gain greater audience, with the advent of all the Apple products (and their competitors).

Thomas Edison originally envisioned the exhibition of cinema as a private exercise. Consumers would watch films in an individual console, much like today.

The length of what we consider commercial entertainment is changing, because the way we watch films is changing. When films were first made, they ran about 10 minutes. Later, they became 20 minute silent films, then grew to 60 minutes, then 120 minutes, and then, boom, "Gone With the Wind"-length. Today, Hollywood films average about 2 hours 30 minutes (not including the trailers).

As feature films become unbearably epic, as people become less patient, and as the desire for enriching stories enlarges, the next wave of filmmakers will be ready to entertain, and the New Chris Nolan will emerge. This book was written for this next wave of storytellers.

I've eliminated all excuses, and I even go further in an epilogue about script format. Unless you're making a *Film School Film* or writing a script for a contest, I doubt you'll actually need it. Take a look if you're insecure about those elements.

But we live in a fearful society, and many of us will take as many training wheels as we can handle. I understand that. I've gone even further. I asked Matthew Helderman and Luke Taylor, creators of the Screencraft & BondIt Short Film Grant to contribute an Afterword. I was fortunate that they read the book, loved it, and said, "yes." These guys are putting their money where their mouth is, literally, awarding up to 10 Grants per year to promising shorts (of up to 25k).

With this Afterword, I have left you NO EXCUSES not to write your short script. When the need for short films explode, you will be ready.

As I complete this book, Chris Nolan himself has just completed a short film as a follow up to the $200 million "Interstellar." A documentary entitled "Quay" about the stop motion animators, The Quay Brothers, filmmakers known for their short films.

Afterword:
Plight of the Singing Frog

By Matthew Helderman & Luke Taylor
Founders, CEOs, Buffalo 8 Productions and BondIt

The first memory I have of a short-film was as a 7-year-old kid, in my parent's basement, watching a Disney movie on. There was a short cartoon prior to the movie.

You may remember this gem yourself — a down-on-his-luck regular-Joe meets a singing frog. Regular Joe sees dollar signs... He rents a theatre and rehearses the frog. It does indeed sing. Average Joe is beside himself. Wealth and power is within his grasp. He'll be packing the theatre for years with this singing frog. But on opening day, no one comes. He offers free admission. Still, no one comes. He offers free beer. Finally, the house is packed. The man has everything he wants… except the frog doesn't sing. Everyone boos and leaves.

Tragically, Average Joe discovers the frog will only sing in his presence. This desperate man goes to every extreme to find a solution, and eventually settles for his previous life of drudgery - albeit with the companionship of a singing frog, unable to turn a profit. He is the only person on Earth who will ever know he has a singing frog.

Looking back on this, I remember being obsessed with the story. It was sad, funny, and suspenseful. The world and characters were unique. It was, as pointed in the book you just read, a "Twilight Zone Short." A commentary on the conviction that you have something to share with the world. *If only they could see what you could see.*

The "Singing Frog" is what every filmmaker thinks he or she has. But no one knows if the toad sings unless there's the proper financing, distribution and advertising for the performance. This cartoon is the plight of the filmmaker today, feature and short. But particularly short, since there are very limited ways to turn a profit after investing time, money and passion into a short film. In other words, if you have a frog that sings, you have little incentive to show him off to the rest of the world. Why rehearse your frog, rent a theatre, promote the heck out of him, knowing no one will show up?

Here's the good news. We're no longer confined to the theatre. Short-form content is literally everywhere, available around the clock, around the world. As feature film producers/executives at a production/ financing firm, we're accustomed to the realities of the business. The landscape has shifted. The paradigms have been turned inside out. No longer does the establishment reign supreme.

Here's even better news. As this exciting book points out, the model is emerging for the short form content. It's not here yet, but it is gestating, and we are proud to say we're at the forefront.

We have established the Screencraft & BondIt Short Film Grant to discover the Next Christ Nolan, Wes Anderson or Richard Linklater, who all started making shorts. Their works were leveraged at festivals, and the success of these shorts catapulted them into professional careers, and more importantly, voices that nourish our culture. "Bottle Rocket" was a Sundance darling financed by Disney (*imagine that happening today!*) as a feature for the first-time director.

Our Grant follows this model, not just in financing ($5,000-$20,000, depending on scale and merit), but in promotion (matching funds for crowd-funding) and guidance (creative development and production guidance). Please check out the guidelines at www.screencraft.org. It is our mission to award 4-10 of these Grants per year.

The shorts that came out of the 1990's are exceptional, and truly shaped the indie feature scene with their irreverence for form, tradition and appeal. Watching these directors segue into feature film masters only further supports the notion that the short form served its purpose: to tell a story well, to perfect the mastery of direction, and to recognize the necessity of resourcefulness that would define cinema for the ages.

As film history insists, a new wave is on the horizon. The micro-budget scene is more prevalent than ever, with roughly 5,000 feature films produced annually. The $10,000 feature film - while incredibly challenging - is now possible, and more frequent than most would have guessed just ten years ago. This budget is less than most of the shorts made in the 90's.

This trend offers an incredible amount of hope to storytellers and filmmakers everywhere. No longer is the garden walled for short-form or long-form. This democratization process has been swift and its effects continue ascending as we witness digital revolutions nearly every other week. Grab a camera, pull together a small team and produce content until you've mastered your craft.

It's easier said than done in regards to becoming the next Hollywood superstar, but physically producing and creating has never been easier than right now.

From Netflix to Twitter, content is being reimagined. Stars being born from YouTube more rapidly than networks and studios. Filmmakers are grasping, they can find an audience through grassroots methods more easily than a mere handful of years ago.

With this flattening of the landscape comes an opportunity to share, discover and deliver. As I look at the opportunities that cross my desk on a weekly basis, they range so dramatically that it's often comical — from Hollywood studio material to indies to shoe-string budgets to a digital distribution platform set to reshape short form content delivery. It's exciting to see this crossroads of opportunity.

Some frogs will sing and some won't. What's important is to provide the platform, like in the Miramax/Sundance era of the 90's, for the ones to sing to be heard. Today, the man with a "Singing Frog" wouldn't need to rent a theatre; he could shoot his amphibian on his iPhone, capture millions of hits, make a good profit and write an autobiography about it. Most importantly, we would all get to enjoy the magical toad.

Formaticus

There's one Greek God no one ever talks about, Formaticus, the God of the Script Format. He ruled with a tight fist. He loved rules and regulations. In college ruled notebooks, he only wrote inside the lines. If he saw anything veering the outside, this dude freaked and took out whole nations with lightning bolts.

People were terrified, as Formaticus struck fear even more deeply... by inventing the script format. He forced everyone in the town of Format to obey his taut laws. Or else.

Alright, I made that up. But you get it, right? We're talking screenplay format. Some of you may not care, others may think the world of it. Either way, we have to cross that bridge.

This portion is most important for the FILM SCHOOL FILM FOLKS (those of you writing a short for a contest need to pay attention here too). The Four Elephants In the Rules.

```
Like most of you, I once had nightmares about
this part. Okay, maybe I didn't have actual
nightmares, but I was at least pretty concerned.

However... the more I wrote scripts, the more I
read scripts, the more I realized this was a
pointless fear.

Eventually, I established my own rules.

Four basic ones to get me through.
```

THE FOUR ELEPHANT RULES

Rule 1) Never write more than two sentences in a paragraph. Doesn't matter if it breaks up an action.

You're writing a screenplay, not an essay. Remember that.

The objective to screenwriting is to communicate your thoughts. Therefore, you want "your INFORMATION to be clear." The more sentences you stack on, the more of a wilderness you create towards communicating your vision. Novice screenwriters send me scripts all the time with literally an entire page without breaks.

I usually space it out (using the space bar).

Anyway...

... you get the point.

More space.

Easier to read.

People don't get confused.

Rule 2) Good grammar means nothing in a script. That's right, no gold stars.

Don't be no grammar Nazi. Why?

It means nothing in the screenwriting world. Read any script online and see what I'm talking about.

Lawrence Kasdan (Empire Strikes Back, Body Heat, Grand Canyon) compares screenwriting to poetry.

Let's see if he has a point:

INT. BOOK STORE - DAY

A man in his fifties on a podium. Delivers his speech. Crowd is rapt.

Now as a poem:

Interior.
Book store.
Day.
A man.
50s.
On a podium.
Delivers speech.
Crowd. Rapt.

They look pretty friggin' identical. Like clones, if I may say so.

Poems also don't follow correct grammar. Think Poem, not essay.

Rule 3) Stay consistent in style.

Paul Schrader famously wrote Taxi Driver in chapters (btw, TD was the hottest script on the market in the mid-70s).

Every director was once attached to it. Spielberg, DePalma and finally Scorsese.

Amazingly, Paul Schrader didn't write INT/EXT or DAY, NIGHT. He wrote TRAVIS BICKLE INTERVIEWS FOR A JOB; that was his logline for the scene.

However, he kept these chapters headings consistent for the whole script.

He didn't suddenly describe scenes the traditional way or break into a song. He kept it with, TRAVIS SAVES A PROSTITUTE.

The readers followed the story.

That's it.

That's all you have to do. Stay consistent.

Whether you write it in Chapters headings, movements, innings, KEEP IT CONSISTENT.

Rule 4) VERBALIZE everything. When you finish your script. Go through it and assassinate as many adverbs and nouns as you can. And then, verbalize everything.

A script is action-based. Verbs are king. Everything is else is a court jester.

For example, instead of

Ronald tenses up like a steel pole.

Ronald steels.

Assassinate as many adverbs, nouns as you can... or convert them into verbs. That's it.

You're not a pro. Just do your best. Don't hurt yourself if you missed a couple.

However, if you're making the Film School Film, you might want to stick to INT and EXT and all that jazz.

Remember, a screenplay is not an essay. It's a screenplay!

The screenplay form is a very young piece of expression. It borrows from other writing forms like A LOT (especially poetry).

In the end, it's nothing more than a blue print. And what is a blue print?

A detailed outline or a plan of action.

What's the most important thing about an outline? It must communicate your plan of action. That's your goal.

You're taking what's in your head and communicating that to the people who will HELP YOU make your FILM.

These four rules is all you need.

1. Two lines per paragraph maximum.
2. Think poem more than essay.
3. Stay consistent in style.
4. Assassinate as many adverbs and nouns as you can; anything left, verbalize them.

I'm not saying, you can misspell freely in your script. That gets irritating and can hurt opportunities.

Definitely spell check your script. Don't NOT spell check.

I said, don't be a grammar Nazi. Good grammar is necessary, within reason.

Placing a period at the end of a sentence, for example (but not always).

If you're not in film school or writing this
script for contest, it doesn't really matter how
you write your script.

As long as people understand what's on the page,
they won't care. Kubrick wrote dialogue where he
was supposed to write action and vice versa. He
deliberately flipped their order.

Woody Allen writes minimal descriptions as he
can. Judd Apatow, same. Like so...

EXT. MUSIC STORE - DAY

Establishing.

As long you are consistent, and not bound by the
rules of film school or a contest, it really does
not matter.

Even professional screenwriters have varying
styles. William Goldman refused to write
sluglines. Lem Dobbs ("Dark City") used to write
with no INT or EXT. Just the location. Ted Tally
wrote character names in the sluglines. There is
no hard rule, except to stay CONSISTENT.
Think of the short screenplay as a poetic blue
print. Close your eyes and imagine what a poetic
blue print looks like.

Now write it. CUT THE EYEBALL, baby!

ABOUT THE AUTHOR

In his 25-year career as a screenwriter, Norith Soth has sold, optioned, or been hired to write countless screenplays and teleplays. Soth has written for Hollywood A-list directors such as Justin Lin ("Star Trek Beyond" and "Fast and Furious 3-6") as well as Sundance favorites, such as producer Brad Miska ("V/H/S" and "Southbound"). With his partner, Mich Medvedoff, Soth started the site www.shortscriptgods.com, that offers anyone the ability to hire a professional to write their short film. It is through this experience that Soth decided to write "Cut the Eyeball." Today, Soth participates in all level of productions, through writing, producing, directing stories he considers "worth telling."

Made in the USA
Lexington, KY
12 January 2018